THE
RUNNING
BACK

THE
RUNNING
BACK

TRUE STORY
FROM THE WHEELCHAIR
TO THE NFL

LEROY COLLINS
FORMER NFL PLAYER – MOTIVATIONAL SPEAKER

For information about this title or to order other books and/or electronic media, contact the publisher:

DC3 Media
www.DC3consulting.com
info@DC3consulting.com

ISBNs
Print: 978-1-7330276-0-1
eBook: 978-1-7330276-1-8

Printed in the United States of America

Cover and Interior design: 1106 Design

In memory of Leroy Collins Sr. (Dad), Curlie Mae Collins (Grandma), and Mary Alice Welch (Aunt)

Contents

Introduction

It was April 24, 1999, and I was sitting in my mother's house in Fredericksburg, Virginia, waiting for my name to be called in the NFL Draft. It was a long and painful day. I remember sitting there waiting, my heart beating out of my chest, wondering what would happen next. Just days earlier my college coach had called me and advised me to withdraw my name from the draft eligibility list. But that was not an option for me. I had a dream and a passion for playing football. I felt this was the perfect time. Coach told me it would never work out, and he wished me luck the way you say "good luck" to a lost cause.

As you'll see, there's never any such thing as a lost cause.

My love of football has always been deep inside me, having rooted itself there during the summer of 1982 when I was just six years old. This passion has propelled me through unthinkable situations where most others would have given up. Football made me feel alive.

o o o

The summer of 1982 would change my life forever. I was six years old and doing the things most kids my age enjoyed. My cousins and I were outside my aunt's house in the housing project playing cops and robbers with water guns. We were out there for hours playing in the heat, using empty detergent bottles as make-shift water bombs. When you live in the projects, you do the best with what you have.

After hours of playing, it was decided that we all wanted to go to the corner store for cold drinks. With only a few pennies in my pocket, I sent my four-year-old brother Ernie back to the house to get more change from my mother. Ernie soon emerged and came back with five more pennies.

The group of us began making our way to the store, playing cops and robbers along the way; my oldest cousin, who was about ten at the time, chasing us with the water gun. He chased Ernie out into the street as I lagged behind. Running and laughing to avoid the water, the other kids didn't see what I saw: a large U-Haul-style truck speeding down the road, much too fast for a neighborhood street. As I tried to stop my brother from unknowingly running directly in its path, it was already too late.

The speeding box truck hit my little brother and tossed him to the sidewalk without even attempting to stop or slow down. Now in the street myself, the truck continued in my direction and, before I even realized what had happened, it hit me as well. The impact was hard and direct, propelling me ten feet in front of the truck as it still continued to lurch forward. I laid in the street, immediately knocked unconscious. While the driver of the truck slowed, he didn't stop. He continued to drive on, running the tires directly over my head, then my chest.

As if that weren't enough, my clothes then snagged on something beneath the vehicle, causing my limp body to be dragged under the truck for a block and a half until my clothes were torn from my body, freeing me. As if all of this weren't horrifying enough, as I now lay a bloody heap in the street, the back tires of the truck ran over my body yet again.

From what I was told, people on the street in those moments were yelling, pleading for the driver to stop as they helplessly watched the terrifying scene unfold. My cousin had witnessed the entire thing and immediately ran to the house to tell my mother. With unmeasurable fear, my mother ran out the door as if reserving a bit of hope that this was all some cruel joke my cousin had been playing on her.

Arriving at the scene of the initial accident (which she thought to be the worst of it) she found Ernie. He was conscious but writhing and crying in pain, unable to get up. As my mother got closer and made her way through the small crowd that had gathered, it was clear to her that his shin bone was completely snapped in half, protruding from his leg. She bent down to him, trying to comfort and console her young son. It was in the midst of this chaos that she inquired as to my whereabouts. The somber response was a simple point of the hand from my cousin, indicating she should look up the street.

Having to temporarily leave Ernie as he lay in pain, my mother ran toward what appeared to be another crowd; this one shrieking, crying, and staring in disbelief. As she approached she heard the frightened sobs and prayers being said by onlookers as she herself cried out to God. "No Lord, no!"

My blood covered the street.

My shoes lay empty.

My mother arrived by my side and immediately fell beside me to pray. Whether she intentionally dropped to her knees or her legs simply gave out, she cried out. "No Lord, don't let him be dead!" She was bargaining with God in a way only a mother can for her baby. "Save my son!" she screamed at the top of her lungs. The rush of adrenaline, shock, and horror took its toll on her in the blink of an eye as she collapsed on the street right next to me, hitting her head on the ground as she fainted. It was there that she would remain, unconscious and lying in my blood until the ambulance arrived. My aunt was on the scene and she was also praying and crying out to God to spare my life. I was lying motionless and unconscious until my aunt screamed out for mercy from God and my eyes flickered open just for a second before they closed once again as I laid motionless.

Back down the street with Ernie, my nine-year-old sister stayed by my brother's side and did her best to console him. Details regarding my condition were traveling fast among the crowd along the street and she knew she couldn't bear to look at me. My injuries were too severe.

As the results of the scene were now abundantly clear, the driver of the truck got out and ran back to see what he had done. He cried, astonished by what had happened. "Somebody help!" he screamed. "Call an ambulance!"

The crowd circled my apparently lifeless body, no one daring to touch me, and most unable to bear the sight of me. They wanted to help but were paralyzed by fear, and no one knew what to do. The people on the street did the only thing they could: they waited for the ambulance to arrive and continued to pray over what seemed to be a hopeless situation.

The police were the first responders on the scene and it was my brother they stopped for first, believing that this was the boy who needed immediate attention. The group of neighbors and onlookers that had gathered around me flagged the officers down, imploring them to attend to me down the street immediately. Upon arrival, the lead officer took one look at me and called for help. "Immediate assistance at Second and Columbia," he cried into his radio. There was no doubt by looking at me that I needed far more than anything anyone there on the street could offer. Checking me for a pulse, he initially couldn't find one. On the second try, my pulse was weak at best.

Given the extraordinary amount of blood it was obvious that I'd lost, the second officer called out on the radio looking for an ETA on the ambulance, urging them to hurry. The response he got was not promising. The ambulance was already on the scene of a head-on collision involving six people a few blocks away. The officers, knowing the auto accident had happened just a few minutes before my own, and being a small town without multiple ambulances available, they knew they had to act fast. It was clear that if I didn't receive immediate care, I would die. More responding officers showed up on the scene, but no ambulance. They did their best to tend to my brother as he was in pain and needed help.

Not wanting to wait another minute, the officers who were standing by with me made the decision to get me to the hospital themselves. Knowing they may have been working against the odds, they carefully loaded me into the back of the squad car; one policeman rode with my mangled body in the back seat while the other turned the siren on and tore down Columbia Street. Negotiating the narrow thoroughfare lined with parked cars and heavy traffic, the officer estimated it would take six to eight minutes to drive the full distance to the hospital. Their goal was to make it in 3 minutes, traveling in excess of 80 mph through seven traffic lights. It was clear that if I was to have any chance of making it through, time was of the essence.

With God on my side, a few of the lights happened to be green until we reached a difficult intersection. The light there was about

Officer Larry Walker

1982

to turn red as we approached and the corner was situated such that it was impossible to see if there was any oncoming traffic. The officer was going to slow down but he knew my situation was dire and he felt a sense of peace as he heard a small voice tell him to keep going. Without giving it another thought he pressed the gas pedal to the floor and got us through the intersection safely, now only two blocks away from the hospital. The officer in the back seat held me, and though still unconscious, I held on to what little life I had.

o o o

Arriving at the hospital, a team of doctors and nurses met the police car, unsure of what they may be presented with. The doctor in charge immediately checked me for a pulse but could find nothing. The officers now second-guessed themselves, wondering if they'd done right by me in transporting me to the hospital themselves. (They would later come to find out that it had taken the ambulance ten minutes to arrive at the scene of my accident and if I'd had to wait, I surely would have died there on the road.) With the one officer reporting the presence of my weak heartbeat just minutes ago, providing the medical team with hope, the doctor started CPR on me, with my heart weakly responding but then fading away once again. A team of doctors and nurses desperately tried again, only to get a second heartbeat that was then also soon lost. Not giving up on me, the doctor tried a third time and my heartbeat held steady enough for me to be rushed into the OR. It was clear to anyone looking at me that I had suffered a fractured skull and I was losing a lot of blood. With all I'd been through it also stood to reason that I was undoubtedly suffering from significant internal bleeding. The medical team knew they had to act fast.

The brain surgeon I would need was located thirty minutes away at Albany Medical Center so I was immediately prepped for the transfer to Albany. As the hospital scrambled to get me stabilized and get me the help I was in dire need of, back at the scene of the accident an ambulance finally arrived. While they were able to attend to the needs of my brother, a second ambulance was called for my mother who still lay unconscious in the street herself, the events of the day clearly too much for any mother to handle.

o o o

My father was a volunteer firefighter and had been working his full-time job at the local gas station just two blocks away from our accident that day. He went about his work completely unaware of what had happened to his boys until a fellow fire-fighter ran into the store to tell him what had happened. His friend had gotten all the details from the police officer that had rushed me to the hospital. While my father had, indeed, heard the call that had come over the scanner, he had no idea it was his own two boys they had been talking about. The firefighter filled him in on my whereabouts and my father immediately stopped what he had been doing and took off running to the hospital on foot. He ran nonstop until he got there.

o o o

As I was loaded into an awaiting ambulance, medical crews continued to work on me. My father was told he would be permitted to accompany me on that desperate ride and as he rushed to be by my side he was shocked by what he found; I was unrecognizable even to my own father. He struggled to believe that the horribly mangled boy in front of him, with a face and head so swollen it was hard to stomach, was the son he had seen playing and laughing just hours before.

While I held on through the ride to Albany, technicians worked tirelessly to do all they could to prepare me for what would come next. Handling my head injury would have to wait. Upon seeing me it was obvious to the surgeons that they would have to wait until the life-threatening swelling went down to fully assess me. My head was easily three times its normal size, outrageously disfigured. The preliminary consensus was that surely I would be brain dead; my head had been fractured so badly my brain could be clearly seen. As far as putting the rest of me back together, I was operated on for hours by various surgeons at Albany Med as my father and my aunt sat in the waiting room doing all they could to pray. By the time all was said and done, it was discovered that I'd endured two broken legs, broken ribs, a crushed pelvis, and such damage had been done as I was dragged under that truck that a skin graft had been necessary on over 40 percent of my body. This was all in addition to the fractured skull. By the time they were done with me I was bandaged from head to toe and still unconscious.

As I was fighting for my life at Albany Medical Center, my brother Ernie was being cared for at Columbia Memorial, the first hospital I had been sent to. My mother was there as they operated on Ernie and addressed the dangerous blood loss he too had suffered. It would be ten hours before my mother would finally see me. In the meantime, my father had yet to see Ernie and he continued to worry about my brother's condition until my mother assured him he was out of surgery and resting. While my father was relieved, he was still very anxious to see my brother.

One can only try to imagine the horror my parents went through that fateful day; the panic, fear, and pain of having two children so critically injured and in separate hospitals was compounded when they each actually saw us. As my mother approached my room after I'd undergone hours of surgery, she paused at the door, unable to walk closer. Staring at me in disbelief even from afar, it was the first she'd seen me, and I was completely bandaged, with wires, tubes, and monitors all sustaining me as I lay motionless and unconscious. Tears streamed down her face as she wondered how this nightmare could come to be. Being a woman of strong faith, she prayed to God for help.

"It's likely that your son will never talk again or be able to function on his own," the doctor told my parents. "You may want to start looking into assisted living facilities and get some options in place," he suggested. This news washed over my mother particularly hard; she was already a frightened, broken woman as the doctor continued to paint a pretty bleak image of my future. "Unfortunately, your son's pelvis was crushed beyond repair; I wouldn't expect him to walk again. I wish I had better news but we'll know more about his overall condition once the cranial swelling goes down and he's out of the coma."

My mother listened to all the doctor had to say, but she refused to fully believe a word of it. She left the room in a daze and went directly to the hospital chapel where she fell to her knees and prayed for God to intervene. She prayed for me night and day, never wavering in her faith.

In the days to come, my mother and father had to juggle themselves between me and my brother. My aunt helped by staying with me while I was still in a coma. Several weeks had passed and my aunts were there by my side while my parents traveled back and forth between hospitals and resting in hotels near Albany Med.

○ ○ ○

The day I awoke from the coma my parents happened to be at Columbia Med spending time with Ernie. The first thing I saw when I opened my eyes was my aunts standing over me. I was immediately frightened, with no idea as to where I was. I couldn't move and I didn't know why. I looked down only to find unexplained bandages and casts holding me down. I thought I began talking but nothing I said made any sense as I mumbled, struggling to find the right words as so many questions flashed through my mind.

My mother was contacted immediately and told that I was not only awake, but that I was talking. As she and my father rushed their way to Albany to be by my bedside, the doctor came in and ushered everyone out of the room in order to get a status on me and run some tests. As the doctor assessed me, my mother waited anxiously outside my door until the doctor was finished and she was allowed to see me. Not knowing what to expect or what was in store for me next, she praised God for the miracle He had just delivered.

Still not fully understanding everything I'd been through, I recall seeing my mother come in the room and I recognized her right away. "Mom, help me," I cried. I couldn't move and I was in intense pain. She rushed to my side, crying and thankful as she grasped my hand and told me she loved me. It wasn't long before I fell asleep and remained asleep for a few days, my family and doctors amazed by everything that had just taken place. They had no explanation for what they'd just witnessed—not only had I woken up, but I was talking.

Any tests that had been previously run had shown I'd suffered severe brain damage, with my brain not even functioning. The medical team truly believed I would remain in a vegetative state.

I left everyone in the hospital scratching their heads that day—everyone except my mother. The longer she had prayed through this whole ordeal the stronger her faith became, along with her belief that God was truly going to see me through. While I'd already defied the opinion of every doctor and seemed to be on the road to recovery, I was far from recovered.

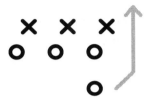

Recovery

With both their boys still recovering from life-threatening situations, my parents were traveling back and forth between hospitals thirty minutes apart. Since I was unable to be moved and was still under close observation my parents requested that my brother be transferred to Albany Med. With staples in his leg and just starting to use crutches, Ernie joined us to share my room—a significant stress now lifted from our parents' shoulders as they would now be with us both. The day I woke up to find Ernie in the bed next to me I was both surprised and confused. *What happened to him? Better yet, what had happened to ME?* As the accident was explained to me on more than one occasion, it meant nothing. I had no memory of anything—including what I'd been doing or who I had even been with that day. All I knew was that I was a broken little boy held together by bandages.

While I remained stuck in bed it wasn't long before Ernie was running all over the room despite the cast on his leg. Becoming restless in that hospital room, he was causing a lot of trouble, but as I watched him from my bed, still bound by bandages and wires and tubes and casts, I wished I could've joined him. In simple terms, it really sucked to be stuck in that bed, and my brother knew that, so he would sometimes climb in with me and hang out when no one was around.

As if being a bedridden captive weren't bad enough, I had bandages that needed to be replaced every day, three times a day—all of the bandages that were covering the delicate skin grafts on nearly half my body had to be changed constantly. It was easily the most painful experience of my life. My mother had to take my brother out of the room when the nurses came in to change my dressings; it wasn't anything for a young boy like him to have to see his brother endure. (God knows it was a lot for me to experience at such a young age myself, but I didn't have much choice.) My legs were broken; but I had skin grafts over 40 percent of my body where skin was taken from my buttocks and placed on my legs to replace what was lost when I'd been dragged beneath the truck—skin and muscle had been literally ripped from my body, mainly from the backs of my legs and all along my back. To call it road burn would be a gross understatement. The bloody bandages stuck to my legs as my body worked so hard to heal itself. I dreaded this necessary daily ritual; it was so painful.

I cried.

I screamed.

It truly felt as if they were pulling the skin off my legs every single day and the whole torturous process took a grueling thirty minutes every single time—sometimes longer if the dressings had managed to dry and stick to me in any one area. It was clear that the nurses felt bad for me, but it was a necessary evil. They

understood the pain I was going through and they tried different techniques to ease some of my discomfort. But regardless of
what they did, there was no mistaking that it still felt like they
were ripping flesh from my body each and every time we had
to go through this process. It pained my mother to see me go
through this every day and it scared my brother. Bad enough to
imagine this being done to you every day, but I had to have this
done *three times a day,* with the morning always being the worst.

o o o

As time passed, my wounds healed and the pain from the
skin grafts under all of those bandages eventually subsided as my
wounds slowly healed. My time at Albany Med was coming to
an end and I was set to be transferred back home to Columbia
Memorial Hospital. While this seemed like a step forward in
my recovery, I now found myself alone in the hospital—it was
time for my brother to go home. My family was seven blocks
away so it was easy for them all to come see me, but at the end
of the day, it was just me in that hospital room. Don't get me
wrong—I had a lot of visitors that brought me a lot of stuff to
try to cheer me up and keep me busy, but the reality was, I was a
little boy still stuck in a hospital. To the relief of my parents, my
wounds were healing to the point where bleeding was becoming
less of a concern, so it seemed we were on the right path. As I
remained in bed, braces kept my legs in place until my broken
bones were fully healed.

o o o

After being in bed for two months it was time for me to
get up and learn how to walk again. Or at least that's what
I thought—if you'll recall, the doctor had told my parents I
wouldn't ever walk or talk again. Knowing I'd already proven

the medical community all wrong as I was already talking, my mother was hopeful and continued to pray for another miracle as she got me up and moving as much as I was able to tolerate. The doctor was skeptical as to whether I would be able to walk but they were willing to give it a shot.

Starting physical therapy, I had to practice the basics—and I do mean *basics*. I had to learn how to stand up all over again. My legs were rigid and seemed to have a mind of their own when it came to fully extending them. No matter how hard I tried, I just couldn't move my legs; they were just so weak and the pain was unimaginable every time I tried to straighten them. The therapist tried to challenge me and she encouraged me to push harder, but there was just no movement. As the days went on, we never gave up and every day I tried to straighten my limbs. I even tried practicing on my own as I'd lie in bed; as painful as it was, I was a determined little kid. In the time I'd been laid up, it was easy to see that I had developed atrophy in my legs and would have to rebuild muscle if I wanted to ever move again. I worked on regaining strength in my legs every day with my therapist until one day, I did it—I stood up. I had to do it by holding onto something, but I did it nonetheless. I stood up. My legs weren't fully extended but I was able to stand and could now at least attempt to move my legs to walk. It was a start.

○ ○ ○

Weeks went by and while I was still unable to walk, the doctors cleared me to go home. After months of living in a hospital room, you can imagine my happiness. I was very ready to get out of that place and back home. Based on what my mother had told me, I knew our apartment was seven blocks away from the hospital, but I had no idea exactly *where* anything was anymore;

I didn't even remember that I'd had cousins who had been to the hospital to visit me. Many things were still foggy in my mind but I was ready to leave; wherever my apartment was, I couldn't wait. I got into my wheelchair (which was now just a part of my new daily life) and was rolled down the hall into the elevator as tears of joy (and nerves) streamed down my mother's face. It was just a few months ago that it seemed there was little hope for my survival, and now we were going home.

o o o

When I got home, my entire extended family was there awaiting my arrival—some I recognized, some I didn't, but I pretended I knew everybody. I was just happy to be home. I soon noticed all the kids in the neighborhood were out playing on the playground and I wanted nothing more than to join them, but I also knew I needed to rest and catch up with my family.

Unable to walk, I managed to get around the house by crawling or using my walker to support me as I dragged my legs along. My mother sometimes carried me but I really wanted to be independent and learn how to do everything myself. Some things obviously required assistance from my mom or dad, like taking a bath, getting into bed, and eating at the table. I was still a kid, after all, but I did try to get myself dressed and would brush my own teeth while standing at the sink leaning on my walker. Some attempts were more successful than others; some days better than others; but I never stopped trying.

o o o

We lived on the second floor of Bliss Towers Apartments, Apartment #224. Our place was on the back end of the tower overlooking the playground and fields where all the kids played. Naturally, I was stuck inside, but I would hear them running around screaming and having fun, making it hard for me to accept I was now limited as to what I could do. I wanted to be out there with them so badly. They played touch and tackle football and I would stand at the window with my walker, wishing I could join them. Being so young and knowing I couldn't play because I was unable to walk made me very sad. I just wanted to be a normal kid. I understood that I'd been in an accident and the doctor said I would never walk again, but I really never took his opinion to heart—I just wanted to walk.

There were many times where I could do little more than sit and cry, asking my mother to fix my legs so I could walk and run like the other kids. My mother was committed to my recovery, and together we practiced every single night to train my body to (hopefully) walk again.

One of our daily exercises involved my mother sitting at one end of the hall in our apartment, holding me up and letting me try to step toward my father at the other end, much as I imagine they'd done with me as a toddler when I took my first steps. I took a few steps on my own but would soon fall, my legs folding from underneath me. Disappointed but determined, we all worked to get me up and do it all over again. I held the wall for support, but there were times I let go and could achieve a bit of a wobbly walk unassisted. One day I finally made it to my father and he turned me around to walk back to my mother. In addition to our daily at-home therapy, my mother rubbed blessing oil on my legs, added it to my bath water, and prayed relentlessly. She did this every day, and I could sometimes hear her praying in her room as she cried and thanked Jesus for all we'd been able to achieve.

o o o

My uncle loved watching football, specifically the NFL. One afternoon in particular, I sat with him watching a game—that was what I believe to be my first time watching a game. To say I fell in love with the sport would be an understatement. I loved how fast the players moved, admired how good they were at catching the ball, and I found the game exciting. With or without my uncle, I continued to watch every Sunday and I especially loved the San Francisco 49ers, and Joe Montana and Roger Craig soon became favorites. Taking notice of my new interest and hoping it would take my mind off my situation, my mother bought me a football helmet. It was just a generic, plain white helmet but I drew the 49ers logo on the side to make it look "real" and I wore that thing all the time, wherever I went. I went to sleep each night with my helmet on and my mother or sister would come and take it off me after I dozed off.

One day I was sitting on the living room floor with my helmet on and an orange slice in my mouth as a makeshift mouthpiece while I watched the 49ers play. It was that day that I told everyone I wanted to play in the NFL. I grabbed onto a chair to stand up, grabbed my walker, and went to find my mother. As I told her of my newly discovered dream, she nodded her head and said, "That's nice," and as any good mom would do, she assured me that one day I just might play in the NFL.

o o o

I was so excited about football that the very idea of one day being able to play made me work even harder in my physical therapy sessions. I knew if I couldn't walk normal I obviously wasn't going to be able to play football, especially at the professional level, so I practiced trying to walk night and day—it became my job. I did every little thing the therapist instructed during our sessions and he also gave my mother little things we should do at home that could rebuild my strength and flexibility. We did it all, and I desperately wanted it to work. To me, it felt like I was getting stronger but my flexibility hadn't really changed much in those weeks I'd been home. I was still unable to straighten my legs causing me to have to bend over at the hip and was unable to stand up straight. There were some days I certainly felt more flexible than others but it felt like every day when I woke up I seemed to start from square one each morning as I was stiff from sleeping, my muscles unyielding to my desperate efforts.

As the days went on, I remember feeling very frustrated; it seemed as if maybe the doctor was right and I was never going to walk like a normal kid again. I went through a period where I wanted to give up and stop trying; I had been working so hard and yet my progress was so slow. My goal to walk on my own now felt like a distant dream. I went back to my walker for a while, but my brother and sister got tired of hearing the noise it made around the house. And while I myself had somewhat surrendered to my condition and felt like giving up, my mother routinely came home from work and immediately prepared me to practice walking. Like any typical kid my age, I'd tell her I didn't feel like exercising, or I wasn't feeling well—I just didn't want to feel disappointed in myself anymore; it was as if my body had betrayed me. My mother remained firm and still insisted I try, so I did it, but admittedly I didn't give it everything I had and she knew it.

In the midst of all this—the cloud of depression and the urge to give up—one night I had a dream that I now believe was my turning point: I dreamt I was outside running and playing with the kids in the neighborhood and I wasn't just playing along—in this dream I was leading the pack as I ran. Nobody could keep up with me! I was smiling, laughing, and happy. I woke up from that simple dream with a new desire burning in my gut and tears of joy in my eyes. I'd always heard my mother praying for me and my brother and sisters, and now I decided it was time to start praying for myself.

From that next day forward, I was committed to practicing day after day with the help of my parents and siblings. Something had come over me and I truly felt like I was going to walk soon—this time for real. It may not have appeared that way by the look of me; my legs were still rigid and I remained bent over at the hip, but something inside me said things were going to change—this was not the end of the road for me. I got to the point where I could stand straight but doing so made it hard to stand in place without wobbling, or to walk without falling. I was able to get my legs to maintain a position that prevented my heels from ever touching the ground even when I used my walker, so I was attempting to walk on my toes with bended knees and frozen hips—not an easy feat and thinking back on it now it must have been quite a sight.

Then one night it all happened.

My mother was putting blessing oil on my legs as she'd done a hundred times and was praying as she lovingly rubbed it over my skin. As she picked me up and placed me in the bath the most amazing thing happened: my legs straightened out. No stretching, no flexibility exercises, no warning or indication— my leg just fully extended. But not just that! My feet began to tingle and I was experiencing a "different" feeling in my toes.

It was like my legs felt alive!

God had heard our prayers and delivered. My mother cried with joy and thanked Jesus. She scooped me up out of the bathtub and I stood there before her straight and tall with no bend in my hips or knees. With both of us caught up in that moment staring at each other in disbelief, I stood there strong and felt ready to walk down the hall as I'd practiced so many times before. My mother dried me off and I started walking out of the bathroom on my own. I walked with a limp, but I was walking with no pain—me, the kid who wasn't expected to walk ever again! My father wasn't home that night when my legs finally straightened out but, boy, wasn't he so surprised? My mother took me to see my aunts and cousins; they were shocked because they'd just seen me the day before and I couldn't walk; we'd spent time on the playground and I had been crawling up the hill so I could get to the top and roll back down. Understandably so, this newest development left my family amazed as they watched me now walk around. When my father came home and saw me walking, he couldn't get to me fast enough as he ran to hug me tight. We had truly been blessed. The vision that had come to me in my dream just a few weeks before was now a reality. I was doing it! I could run and play with the other kids! My mother kept a close eye on me, but I was having the time of my life—I never wanted that day to end. I could see my bedroom window from the playground and can remember all the hours I looked out, watching the kids run and play, having fun. All I ever wanted was to walk, and I did. With hard work and the healing power of God, I stood up, walked, and was now outside running.

A few days later my mother brought me to the doctor for a checkup. The last time I'd seen this doctor I was in a wheelchair and using a walker. This was the guy who believed I'd never walk again, not from lack of faith, but based on medical facts. When he saw me walking into his office, he stopped in disbelief.

"Leroy, is that really you? You are truly a miracle from God." This was the man who had seen me at my worst. He was there when my lifeless bleeding body laid there on a gurney and they had little hope of bringing me back to life. He looked at me in amazement with tears in his eyes. He had been unsure if I'd talk again, but he had been very confident that I would never walk as I once had. As it was, it had been a shock for him to hear me speak as I came out of my coma, so it was now really difficult to comprehend the fact that he was seeing me walk into his office. Lost for words, tears streamed down his face. "God has a plan for you," he said.

○ ○ ○

I was so happy to be out playing with other kids—you have no idea. And oddly enough, I was now running faster than some of the kids who had outrun me in the past. I limped when I walked, and there was no pain, but my mother didn't allow me to play some of the games the kids were engaging in. She was determined to monitor me and make sure nothing happened to me again. She had felt so bad for so long, blaming herself for my brother and me getting run over by the truck. It now became routine that if she had to go inside for something, I was to go inside with her. She didn't trust anyone anymore. (My cousins were supposed to be watching us on the day of the accident.) My mother kept a close eye on us at all times; it was a little frustrating from a kid's perspective, but soon became a way of life.

○ ○ ○

One day I received a signup sheet through school for Pop Warner football—I wanted to play football so bad. As predicted, my mother wouldn't sign my permission sheet no matter how much I begged and pleaded. "You'll get hurt," she'd say, or, "You're not ready to play, it's too soon." I was devastated. I couldn't understand her reasoning—I was running faster than most of the kids in the neighborhood and they were on the team! My father tried to come to my defense and persuade my mother to relent, but she stood firm.

"How will I get to the NFL if you don't let me play football?"

"You'll play one day, Leroy, but not this year," she said.

I sat out that season, but I knew I was going to play next year and nothing was going to stop me.

First and 10

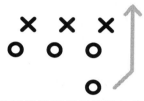

The second season of football came around and again I received a permission slip. "Mom, do you think I could play this year? I really feel ready," I said.

"You know I can't have you getting hurt, Leroy," she said. "This is a dangerous sport, come on. Not this year. Wait one more year."

I tried to assure her that I wouldn't get hurt because I'd been working out all year with my uncle, specifically to train for this season.

She still refused to sign the permission slip.

I didn't want to miss another season; I believed I was ready to play. I had been playing tackle football with the kids in the neighborhood and had dominated. "But Mom," I said, "I know I'm better than all the kids out there and they're on the team! I can run faster than they can!" My mother wouldn't listen; she believed that if I got one hit to the head I could really be set back and permanently injured.

I was so upset I cried for two days straight. The deadline for sports physicals was approaching and I could feel myself starting to panic. I went to my uncle and asked him to sign my permission slip because I didn't want to miss the physical, which I needed to pass if I ever wanted to play. He agreed to sign the permission slip, which made me very happy—I was finally going to be on a football team. The coach was familiar with my accident and seemed unsure as to why I was showing up, but my uncle assured him I was fine and ready to play. I had passed the physical and made the weight requirement, so I was cleared to play football. I wanted to play running back like Roger Craig or throw the football like Joe Montana. I was so excited, ready to show everyone I was ready to play—except my mother. I couldn't tell her I was on the team. She didn't want me to play so I knew I'd have to make sure she didn't find out.

The next day we had to get fitted for our uniforms and we were assigned positions. Coach told me I was going to be a lineman. I remember being really confused about what my duties were. I knew how Roger Craig ran the ball and I knew how Joe Montana threw the ball, but outside of that, I had no clue. And back at home I had to come up with a plan to hide my uniform each day. When I'd come home from practice I'd hide it on the back staircase next to the fire door. Those stairs were rarely used so it felt as if my equipment was safe there (for now).

For the first two weeks of practice, I got a ride from a family member or friend, thinking that was keeping me in the clear with my mother—until the one day she showed up toward the end of practice. I was so shocked to see her, I froze in my tracks as she did not look happy. She approached my coach directly and made it clear that she hadn't given me permission to play, so how was I on the team? The coach danced around the fact that he had received a permission slip with her signature, as she went on to explain that she'd never signed any such thing and she wanted me off the team. She went on to explain about the accident my coach was already aware of. He said that he had noticed I walked and ran with a limp and wondered was I going to be fit to play. In the end, after their unexpected conversation, I had to turn in my uniform—I was so sad. As we went home that day, she lectured me again on how I was not allowed to play and warned me not to do it again.

The pain I felt that day was like getting hit by a truck all over again. I loved football. In all those days I'd been unable to walk; all I ever thought about was playing football. Now I could walk, but my mother's fear over what might happen was preventing me from playing, and that was a hard fact to deal with. I asked my dad to talk to Mom and I would also talk to my uncle and ask him to convince her to see things my way. I even talked to the coach and asked him to plead my case, which he eventually did for me. A week or two had passed since I'd been "found out" and the team was now preparing for their first game. Coach assured my mother that if I were permitted to be on the team, he would look after me. I wouldn't play much, and I would be playing lineman. In the end, my coach won her over with talk of learning teamwork, relationship-building, and boosting confidence, along with his personal promise to keep me out of any dangerous situation.

And so, my mother finally agreed to let me play football just in time for the first game. Sunday morning came around and I was so excited to receive my game jersey—I felt like a big shot. As I stood in line for my name to be called they were wrapping things up and I realized I hadn't heard my name. "Coach, I didn't get a jersey. You never called my name," I said, my inner anxiety rising. He looked through the boxes and bags but came up empty; he couldn't find another jersey. He had a bunch of pants but no extra jerseys.

"Leroy, I'm sorry . . . I guess I took your name off the roster when your mother took you off the team weeks ago. I only brought just what I thought I needed for today." The disappointment I felt hearing those words was heavy. One of the other coaches offered to make the twenty-minute drive to Coach's house to get my jersey. When he returned, I was so excited—I was going to be in my first real football game. There were people in the stands ready to watch, and it was the most thrilling feeling. While I'd always played tackle football with my brother, cousins, and friends, it had always been fun, but this was a new level for me. I was electric with nervous excitement.

The game started, and I sat on the sideline cheering my team on, waiting for my chance to get in the game. Time was passing by and I waited. Halftime came around and they handed out orange slices. I think I ate a whole bag of oranges while I waited as patiently as I could. I kept a slice in my mouth as a mouthpiece just like I'd done before. Halftime was over, and I went back on the sideline to wait for my chance. Before I knew it, time on the clock had run out and the game was over.

I never got a chance to play.

My emotional deflation quickly gave way to sadness. My mother and cousins had come to watch me play. I walked to my mother with tears in my eyes. "It'll be okay, baby . . . your team won and there will be many more games," she said as she hugged me. My coach saw I was upset.

"We'll make sure you play next week," he offered as condolence. I knew I had missed a lot of practices and had to make those days up to learn the plays. Hearing Coach's words of encouragement set my mind straight and I focused my excitement on practicing and getting prepared for next Sunday's game.

I went to practice the next week (still excited) looking forward to playing but found myself sitting on the sidelines, just like at the game. The coach would come over every so often to show me how to stand or demonstrate how to hit the bag. What's happening here, I thought? I wanted to practice with the team! Coach tried to set my mind at ease, explaining that I first had to learn proper technique in order to be accurate (and safe). I quickly picked up what Coach was showing me and was ready to line up in front of another player; this was to be my very first time lining up on the field, with my equipment on, facing another player. I was very nervous, but I was eager to impress everyone. As I lined up, Coach told me which guy to block, so I was clear on my objective. At the sound of a whistle, the quarterback went through his cadence, then hiked the ball. My direct opponent ran into me, we hit heads and I jammed my fingers, and he ran past me to make a tackle, but all my anxiety was now gone and I was ready to do it again.

By the time our second game day rolled around, I was as ready as ever but very excited and still nervous. When the game started I was on the sideline jumping up and down, cheering for my team, waiting (again) for my chance to get on the field. As we went into halftime I hadn't had the opportunity to play yet, but I did eat a whole lot of oranges. Finally, with two minutes left in the game, Coach called on me. "Leroy, block your guy and don't let him get to the quarterback or running back." I ran out onto that field with a renewed sense of purpose as I stood in the huddle, then broke to line up in front of my guy.

"Hike!" called the quarterback. Moved largely by adrenaline, I lunged out, but missed my guy; he'd sidestepped me, and I fell to the ground with everyone else falling on top of me—I was at the bottom of the pile. As you can imagine, my mother was out on that field before anyone knew it to see if I was okay. I told her I was fine, and I didn't let her concern bother me—It had been fun, except for me missing my block.

Getting back to the sideline, I felt like a real member of the team when I heard Coach exclaim, "Open your eyes next time you block someone, Collins!" We laughed and I promised him I would. I was just so happy to be out there. I had played in my first game and walked away unharmed. And my season went on like that for the remainder of that year; I didn't play or practice much. I totaled maybe ten minutes all season. I wanted to play more but Coach routinely put me in with only a few minutes remaining in the games.

With my first full season now securely under my belt, I planned to work hard over the winter and summer and come back next year better than my last. My mother even seemed like she was happy that I'd played (maybe more relieved that I walked away unscathed). She remained cautious but seemed pleased that I was part of a team and I was loving it. She enjoyed watching me build relationships and she saw that I was learning a few things about discipline and respect. I was glad to be on the team—I just loved suiting up on Sundays to play. (I just wish I could've had a little more game time.) It was frustrating to stand on the sideline, knowing I still had so much to prove. I made a point of talking to my coach after the season was over.

"I'm definitely playing next year and I'm going to work hard to do better."

"Just work hard and don't ever quit. Everything else will fall into place," he said.

So, I did just that, and after sticking to my personal training plan, I was ready to play some football. I entered my second season looking for things to be different. I believed I was running faster and moving better; I still had a slight limp but it was better than it had been the previous year. I was hoping to play running back this next year but when we lined up for our uniforms and received our positions, the coaches made me a lineman for the second season. "But Coach, I was faster this year so can I play a different position."

"I don't want you to play another position because I can't have you getting hurt." It wasn't until then that I understood that my mother had made it clear to my coach: when it came to me, his sole responsibility was to be sure I didn't get hurt on the field. Best way to accomplish this mission: limit my game time to instances where we were winning by a mile or had only a few minutes left on the clock.

Although my second season was playing out like my first, I was now armed with information and more determined than ever. I played only a handful of minutes the first few games of the season and I really needed something good to happen because I was starting to get angry with the game I loved.

During our fourth game of the season we were playing a tough team known for beating us every year—It was a very important game for us. We were winning by a few points and there were only a few minutes left in the game. It never really occurred to me that I might get in the game, given the close score. I was wrong. When the offense went out, Coach told me to go out there with them, reminding me to open my eyes when I blocked. I ran out there, stunned and wanted to do the best job of my life. The quarterback yelled. "Hut-hut-hike!" I lunged out, hit my guy, and held my block like I was supposed to, but it was in the very next play that everything changed for me. The quarterback yelled, "Hike," and the running back went for the ball but fumbled it. The ball was rolling along on the ground before the other team picked it up and started running the other way. I saw our guy try to tackle him but miss.

"Go! Go! Go tackle him," I heard from the sideline. I turned and started running after him as fast as I could. I ran past all my teammates who were already chasing him, and I caught him at the five-yard line. Cheers immediately erupted as I was consumed by the excitement of high-fives.

I did it!

I finally did something that changed the outcome of a game. Our defense held them until time expired and we won the game. We finally beat the one team that had been beating us for years, and I had played a part in our victory. I was so proud of myself; everybody around me shared my excitement. "Collins, I never knew you were that fast! We could've used that speed all year!" cried Coach.

Touchdown

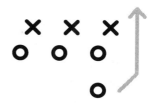

It was at the very next practice that Coach said he wanted to try me out at wide receiver. He lined me up with the other receivers to see if I could catch, and I was doing pretty well. I'd learned a lot by playing with the boys in the neighborhood. We'd always played with kids older than us so while it may have been more challenging, it was also fun. I was ready for whatever the coach was going to throw at me. I ran the route Coach instructed and caught the ball. I kept running routes and catching passes. I was doing so well he told me I was no longer an offensive lineman. In my eyes, that good news meant my dream of going to the NFL was closer to being realized. I practiced all week as a wide receiver in preparation for next Sunday's game day. A nervous stomach was being pretty routine for me but I didn't want to mess up my opportunity and possibly get moved back to lineman. The game started and I didn't get put in right away. I paced the sideline waiting for my chance to get in.

Coach called me over and told me to stand next to him. "Stay with me, you're going in," he said. I followed closely as he walked up and down the field following the ball and calling out plays. Finally, two minutes into the second quarter, I heard, "Leroy, go in at right receiver." I limped to the huddle as the coach came in, called a play and looked right at me. "He's going to throw the ball to you, so run fast like you did the other day." My heart started beating so hard I thought it was going to come out of my chest. We broke the huddle and I ran to the wide receiver position for my very first time in a real game, with the knowledge that the ball was coming to me.

I coached myself through those next few moments. "Catch the ball, catch the ball . . ."

I listened to the quarterback yell out his cadence; the play was on two. He said, "Down, set, hut!" I jumped offside on the first sound. The referee blew the whistle and we had to move back five yards. I had been so hyped-up, I'd jumped the gun. As we went back to the huddle I thought I'd messed it up for sure, having blown my opportunity to catch the ball, but Coach came in and noticed my apparent despair.

"Calm down, it's alright. We're gonna run the same play, this time on one." We broke the huddle and ran to the line of scrimmage. I took my position, not as nervous this time, but now focused and ready to catch the ball.

The quarterback yelled, "Down, set, hut!" and everything around me went silent—all I could hear was his cadence and my breathing. Before I knew what my legs were doing, I'd taken off running. I ran past the defender, turned around, and spotted the ball coming at me. (I actually had to slow down and go back a little to get the ball.) The second that ball was in my hands I could hear the crowd cheering. As I turned to run down the field, the defender grabbed my jersey and tried to bring me down. I ran for the end zone; trying to shake him off I kept fighting, pulling, and turning. Then I shook him loose and it was just me and the end zone—I couldn't believe it—I was about to score my first touchdown. So many things were running through my head as I ran down that field. I thought about how I had been in a wheelchair (and later a walker) watching other football players run for a touchdown. I thought about how I'd played an entire year as an offensive lineman despite being one of the fastest on the team. I felt invincible as I ran for that touchdown. I ran to the sideline where my team hugged me, and my coach slapped me on the back, picked me up, and told me he knew I could do it. I looked to the crowd to see my mother cheering for me and clapping; she looked so happy. Putting my hands over my face, I started to cry, and I just let it go. This was the happiest day of my life.

○ ○ ○

We ended up losing that game but I couldn't wipe the smile off my face. The next practice, Coach wanted me to play a little running back as well. Coincidentally, my cousin was the starting running back at the time, and Coach let me share time with him. I went over a few plays in practice with the coach and he told me I might be running a few plays from the running back position in the next game. I was thrilled to now have the chance to run like Roger Craig did with the 49ers. All this time, I'd been dreaming of being a running back and here I was.

It was Sunday and I went into the game day feeling a little different then I'd felt in previous games; I felt a little more in control rather than like a handicapped little boy whose mommy didn't want him to get hurt. I still walked and ran with a limp, but I didn't feel different from anyone else. I felt like "one of the kids" and I felt I had something definite to prove because I believed I had places to go. The coach called me to come in the running back position. This was my first time lined up as running back in a real game, although I'd done this many times in our neighborhood games. I was nervous, but I felt in control. We ran to the huddle and the coach called a play for me; it was a toss sweep—my job was to run to the sideline as fast as I could and then turn up and head for the end zone. We broke the huddle and headed to the line of scrimmage. The quarterback went through his cadence and everything around me went silent—all I could hear was his voice. The center hiked the ball and tossed it to me. I caught the ball and ran as fast as I could to the sideline, trying to turn up. I was tackled but close to a first down. (I was hoping to get another chance because I wanted another touchdown.) We ran a play and got a first down. I looked over to the sideline, hoping the coach wasn't taking me out because I wanted to run again. Coach came to the huddle and called another play for me—one we'd worked on all week. This was an up-the-middle handoff where I had to go to an assigned hole. I lined up and thought about how Roger Craig ran the ball. He ran fast and hard with high knees, so I was going to run the ball like that—very aggressive. The quarterback said hike. I ran to the hole, and the quarterback handed me the ball and the lineman made a hole for me. I ran fast and hard; I didn't want to be tackled. I believed if I did well, or maybe even scored a touchdown, the coach might let me stay at running back. I made it through the line of scrimmage and I ran past the linebackers. I now had just one guy to beat. I faked him to the outside and then cut it back in and off to the races. I made that one guy miss and was running for my second touchdown! I scored and was very grateful for my linemen. I ran the ball, barely touched, and I'd scored a touchdown! While I'd been a lineman just a few weeks ago, I hadn't played much, but now understood the importance of a lineman doing his job and blocking; it made my job a lot easier when I ran the ball.

I switched back and forth from running back and wide receiver for the remainder of the season, scoring a few more touchdowns, helping my team win a few games. This was a very exciting year for me, my parents, and the coaches. I went from an offensive lineman only playing a few minutes a game to a starting wide receiver also playing running back and scoring touchdowns. My mother had experienced a few scary moments along the way, when I was tackled and all the guys were piled up on top of me. She wasn't afraid to run out onto the field and pull guys off me. She was afraid I might be injured under the pile. I was unharmed, and she was told to stay off the field and let the coaches handle it. As someone who went through all my mother had, it was difficult for her to let anybody handle anything when it came to her boys. She conceded and followed the rules after that but make no mistake about it—her voice was heard.

I was so proud of my accomplishment. I just never stopped working and believing I could do greater than my current situation. I always believed I would run the football for touchdowns in a real game, even when I had been unable to walk. I'd always envisioned myself running a football and scoring touchdowns. I hadn't ever imagined the specifics but I'd always known it would happen. I'd scored not by running the ball but because I ran after someone else who was running with the ball—to think I'd once been in a wheelchair, told I'd never walk again, but yet here I was outrunning others on the football field? If I had allowed my circumstances to get in the way of my vision I would not have accomplished anything. I still would have been in that wheelchair, still using a walker. I would've still been looking out the window, wishing I could've joined the other kids. But because I fought through my challenges, I faced my limitation head on. I knew there was so much more I wanted to do.

Thinking back to the time I'd struggled to get around, I realize just how little I really knew about perseverance and facing challenges. I only ever knew that I was going to do everything I could to get what I wanted. In those times when I wasn't happy in the place I was in, I did things to change my situation.

It all started with a dream.

A dream to walk around without any assistance.

A dream to play with the other kids and a dream to play football. Through hard work and the right amount of faith, dreams can come true.

○ ○ ○

I walked away from that season with my head held high. I had no regrets and I wouldn't have changed a thing. I'd started the season as an offensive lineman, then was moved to receiver, where I scored my very first touchdown. Then my dream to play running back came to fruition and I went on to score many touchdowns. I received an award for most improved player of the year.

With the season now over, my wait for next football season immediately began; it couldn't come quick enough. Before that next season started, Coach told me I might be too big to play football that year. I was at the same weight as last season but

I was a year older, so that made things difficult. There was no modified football program so I either had to lose weight or sit out for two years until I was able to play junior varsity. I was totally against that, so I tried to lose weight. I was working hard and I was getting there. I was running hills, working out with my uncle, and running stairs. There wasn't anything I wouldn't do to lose those few pounds I needed to shed before sign ups.

During the time I'd been training, my uncle noticed something—my limp had disappeared! I'd been walking around limp-free and hadn't even noticed it until he said something about it. While it had never slowed me down (that I thought, anyway) I do believe I was now even faster without the limp.

I was almost ready for my third season of football. I'd trained very hard for that year and I was running faster than ever. I was so excited I could hardly wait. Until the unthinkable happened. One day my family decided to just up and move to Florida—mere weeks before football season.

Florida

Unbeknown to any of us kids at the time, our father was having some problems in Hudson and for the safety of us all, a quick decision was made to seek a fresh start in Florida, where we had extended family. We didn't know the exact nature of Daddy's situation, but we knew we were getting out of Hudson in a hurry. Probably more upsetting to me than leaving the only town I'd ever lived in, was the fact that it was a week before the start of football season. I had trained so hard in anticipation and now I wasn't sure if I was even going to be able to play once we got down south.

Everything really happened very fast. One afternoon we had all been outside playing with our cousins and friends, running the ball and doing what kids do without a worry or a clue. Then later that night, with no warning, no talk of a plan, we found ourselves rushing around to pack the car up. "Mom, what's going on? Where are we going?" I tried asking.

"I just really need you kids to all pitch in right now, Leroy. We're in a bit of a hurry, baby. Here's a bag for you, and pass these on to your brothers while I help the girls," she said, handing me some garbage bags while I struggled to put things together in my mind. "Well don't just stand there, c'mon, Roy! Put your clothes and whatever treasures you've got in your bag and help your brothers do the same, okay, baby?"

It was clear we were heading out, just like that, but as I hurried (it was clear by Mom's actions that time was of the essence), I still didn't know "where" we were going yet. We all worked frantically, stuffing as many personal belongings into overstuffed plastic bags while Mom packed up all the food she could manage to fit into her sixteen-foot brown-and-tan station wagon (you know the old-school kind), wedging everything in to still leave room for the six of us kids and herself and my dad. My baby sister Danielle was strapped into her car seat surrounded on all sides by all our personal worldly possessions. And while it seemed like a lot was in that car, seeing it packed floor to ceiling, we were leaving our "big stuff" behind; with no time or financial resources to call a U-Haul or rent a truck, we were abandoning the furnishings that had actually made that apartment our home.

So, there we were, in the middle of the night, Mom encouraging us to all find our places in the very back to settle in for what would be a long road trip. Through her tone and the urgency, we sensed in her actions, we knew it wasn't the time to ask a lot of questions, but rather to do as we were told. Me, my two brothers, and two sisters rode in the back together (back in the days before seat belt laws existed and kids could pile into the back of any car or pickup truck bed), and as luck would have it, with those enormous station wagons of the time, the hatchback provided just enough room for the five of us to sleep. As far as we knew (which wasn't much) we needed to get out of Hudson and we were all unsure if we were permanently moving to Florida or just going to visit. Aside from whatever plan Mom had in mind, we kids knew nothing until we reached our final destination.

After a full day of travel, we arrived in the Sunshine State where our extended family comprised of aunts, uncles, and cousins welcomed us to their house in Florida. I don't think we had been there five minutes before I asked about whether they had a football team and who I could talk to about playing. When we'd left upstate New York, football season had been just about to start so I knew it was close to starting in the south as well and I wasn't going to miss any opportunity to play.

Not having a place of our own arranged just yet, we lived with my grandmother and uncle until we were able to find a place of our own. Grandma had a small house when you considered the number of people living there. It was a three-bedroom, one-bathroom house with members of our extended family already living there. It was overcrowded before my family even arrived on the scene, to say the very least. I'm not going to sugarcoat it. It was rough with my grandmother already having other family members staying with her, and then we show up. My grandmother has a huge heart and she loves her family so even with twenty people living in a three-bedroom house she seemed to somehow make it work. Things did get hectic at times with a lot of people in a small space. So we kids spent a lot of time busying ourselves outside the house, even if that meant just playing ball out in the yard.

Mom started looking for a job right away while my grandmother watched us, but her plate was already so full with so many other kids to look after that she never really had time for herself, and that really both bothered and worried Mom. So, while we were all anxious to find a place of our own, it just wasn't realistic right away. "Just hang on a little longer," Mom would tell us. "We're going to get our own place soon and things will settle down. In the meantime, try to help out and keep your brothers and sisters outta Grandma's hair, okay, Roy? Can you do that for me?" she'd ask, kissing me on the forehead, giving me that extra assurance that we were gonna be alright.

As some time went on and even we kids started to feel the stress of not having a place of our own, we couldn't help but continue to wonder why we had to be in Florida. "Why'd we move, knowing we didn't have a place to stay?" one of us would routinely ask, sometimes grumbling but often being offered the same vague explanation.

"I've told you kids . . . Daddy just got himself into a little trouble and it was best for us to leave for a while." No matter how hard we pressed we never got much more out of her than this but she'd place a gentle hand on our shoulders as she tried to explain all that should ever be shared with children our age. "It's hard to explain, Leroy, and maybe someday you'll know the whole story. But for now, what's important is that we're together and we're safe. Right, baby? Just hang in there with me and help your brothers and sisters do the same. You're my strong boy and I'm counting on you." She smiled and pulled me close, her sweet smell instantly soothing any doubts I had.

A couple of weeks went by and Mom found a job; more than one, I would later come to learn. One thing about my mother that was (and still is) undeniable, was her determination to provide for her children, even if that meant working long hours doing odd jobs like cleaning, working in the potato fields, and even picking peanuts (something she's still a bit embarrassed by, but when you have six young mouths to feed, you do what you have to do). As an adult myself now, knowing what she did for us feels bittersweet. While I don't like to think of how hard she must have been working to keep our heads above water, it's heartwarming to think that she was working so hard out of love for us. So, although she was working multiple jobs, and then coming home after long hours and having to be "Mom," our living arrangements had yet to change. We were still between my grandmother's and aunts' houses. (Let's be real for a minute and consider how much it takes to feed and clothe six children, even for someone with a traditional 9–5 job making a decent wage. And trying to find an apartment that would not only accommodate seven of us but be within Mom's limited budget??) But staying with our relatives, even from a kid's perspective, felt like we were wearing out our welcome. My mother never really felt comfortable descending upon the homes of others, even if they were family. She didn't like relying on someone else for shelter, especially given the fact that she had six kids; she knew we could be a handful. So, she searched hard for a place to stay.

Mom finally found an apartment on the other side of town just five miles from my grandmother, and we were so excited to hear we'd be moving in to a place of our own. Maybe things would feel "normal" again. Don't get me wrong: we were all very grateful for the opportunity to stay with family but we all knew it was time to move forward.

Our new apartment was in a quiet little community and we had three bedrooms, one bathroom, a kitchen, and living room. It wasn't much, but it was ours and we were happy to be there, finally in our own space.

I was going to be starting the seventh grade in our new town and I wasn't sure what to expect, being "the new kid" so I went into school expecting the worst. Aside from typical new school anxiety, I was also feeling very self-conscious about the appearance of my legs, still showing clear signs as a result of the accident. I had huge scars on both the fronts and backs of my legs that I felt looked gross. I did everything I could to keep them hidden by wearing tall socks or even routinely wearing pants despite the hot Florida temperatures just so nobody would see them.

I soon discovered that football season had already started and it was too late for me to sign up. I was upset that I couldn't play for the school team, but that didn't stop me from playing tackle football outside the school with a few guys. I was still playing really well and everybody always wanted me on their team, complimenting me by saying I was superfast and could catch like Jerry Rice. The crazy thing was that these were guys who had no clue that I'd just learned to walk again only two years prior. I may not have been able to play for the school team that year, but that didn't stop me from going to every practice to learn as much as I could through observing, listening to the coaching, and playing with my own group of guys.

o o o

School was going well and I was starting to adjust to the way they did things in Florida, making fast friends. The other kids thought I was just the coolest, being that I was from New York. When you tell somebody you're from anywhere in New York state, they immediately think you're from NYC, so I just let them think what they wanted. Hudson was right outside of New York City so I never felt the need to say anything to correct them.

After school one day the bus dropped us off at the edge of the community. Me and my brothers had to cut across the neighborhood to get to our apartment. You can imagine our surprise when we walked through the door to see that our father was there! We were so happy; we hadn't seen him much since our arrival in Florida.

o o o

Everything was good at home, at least in my eyes. We didn't see Grandma much after we moved because my mother worked a lot and we only had one car. We didn't see our extended family much either (aunts, uncles, or cousins) after we moved. We mainly stayed in our little community, with few visitors aside from a friend who lived nearby.

There wasn't much to do in our new neighborhood, but there was a big grass field where we played football and kickball. At night, my brother and sisters would gather to watch TV or play board games. We didn't have much in the way of furnishings either—We had a couch, a chair, a small coffee table, and a TV, VCR, and a radio. We had three mattresses, one of which my mother and baby sister shared. Two of my sisters slept on the second one, and me and my two brothers slept on the third. Half the stuff we had in our apartment had been given to us, and we were grateful because we'd started off with nothing but an empty refrigerator that came with the place. The TV we had was small, but it did its job along with a stack of movies for the VCR, and my mother loved the radio because she could listen to her gospel music. We didn't have much, but we were happy, and we were together. My father would pop in every now and then, and we were happy when we got to see him since he never stayed on a regular basis.

One day when we came home from school my mother was sitting in the living room crying. I sat down beside her, putting my arm around her. "Mom, what's wrong? Did something happen?" She leaned in and hugged me tight.

"It's nothing to worry about, Leroy. Everything's alright," she said, attempting to dry her eyes. But I knew something was bothering her or else she certainly wouldn't have been in the living room crying all alone. My brother Ernest was the first to notice what was really going on.

"Mom, where's the TV?" he exclaimed.

"Maybe you kids should sit down," she suggested gently. "Your father was here and I'm afraid he borrowed some things for a while."

"More than just the TV? Like what? Why?"

"The TV, VCR, and the radio."

"Well, where did he take them?"

"I'm not sure, kids. I'm sorry."

"Well, is he bringing them back?" I asked.

"No," she said, "he's probably already sold them."

My oldest sister stood up like she was demanding answers. "Why would he sell our stuff?"

That was when Mom told us that our father was dealing with "some issues." My brothers and sisters and I were so confused. How could he steal those things from us? My mother went on to explain.

"Look," she said matter-of-factly, "Daddy still loves us all but he's going through some personal problems." She gazed over each of our faces and could see we still weren't quite getting the specifics we were looking for. "Daddy has an addiction and is going to need help."

Along with the TV and VCR, he'd taken a few pieces of my mother's jewelry, along with the money my mother had specifically set aside for the utility bills. My mother didn't really want to tell us he'd stolen our TV and left us with nothing, but for one thing, it was really obvious that something we'd all enjoyed was gone, and secondly, Mom had no other choice because the TV wasn't coming back and she didn't have the money to get us a new one any time soon.

It seemed that our lives had changed that day, and none of us had seen it coming. So, there we sat, in the house with no TV or radio and a hurt mother, while the six of us children tried to wrap our minds around the fact we truly had an absentee father.

A week after my father had looted us, the electricity went out. I assumed the power was out in the whole neighborhood, but soon realized it was just our apartment. The money my father had taken the previous week was what she had socked away for the electric bill. Seeing as how she was unable to pay it, they turned our power off. We lit candles all throughout the house and I remember my mother being very upset, crying and praying. We did everything we could to console her but she just was too broken and ashamed to have to deal with this. She felt like she'd let us down and like there was no way out. We lived without lights for about two weeks and our water was soon turned off as well. My mother bought a grill so we could eat since the stove was not working. She only had enough money for food, bottled water, charcoal, and lighter fluid. Unfortunately, she did not have enough money for the lights and water and soon didn't have enough for rent. It all ultimately came down to her feeding us, or getting the lights and water turned on. She was our only provider and she worked so hard to make sure that we had food. We had to go to relatives' houses to take baths, which we only did a few times, because my mother didn't like that we had to go someplace other than home. The community we lived in had a laundromat, so at least we were able to wash our clothes. Mom had to work extra hours because she was afraid she wasn't going to have enough for rent that was due within the following week.

o o o

Mom was gone a lot trying to make ends meet and my father was still nowhere to be found, so my eldest sister babysat us often. Mom came home from work one day and there was an eviction notice on the door—we had one week to get the water and lights restored or we would have to move. The rent also happened to be due on the same day. It was obvious to us all that my mother felt really hurt and very alone. She was undoubtedly embarrassed that she felt she had allowed this to happen. My siblings and I just wanted my mother's pain to end. My oldest sister tried to help the situation by telling Mom that while we didn't have a TV or lights, we had each other, and we could make it through anything. I think that helped Mom feel better, knowing that her kids were feeling positive and in good spirits. My oldest sister always made sure we had something fun to do together under the candlelight, playing board games like Candy Land and card games like Uno with us. My sister was an extension of my mother; she too wanted us to feel safe and forget about the TV and electricity, and just feel loved. What she did worked night after night as we would look forward to gathering together to play games. I believe that time we spent in the dark made our bond and faith all the stronger.

o o o

My mother felt it was time to move back to New York. We didn't have the means and resources to stay in Florida and it seemed like everything was up against us. My mother was ready to leave Florida and vowed to never find herself in this position again. My father was missing in action and was unaware that my mother had even made the decision to move back to New York. Unfortunately, he sort of disappeared after he took the TV and the rent money. My mother gathered us around one day and asked us how we would feel about moving back north to New York. All of the children screamed with joy at the same time. We were so happy to hear this new development and couldn't wait to see our friends and family back in New York.

"Is Daddy coming with us?" my oldest sister asked Mom.

My mother looked at us with tears pooling in her eyes. "I'm sorry, kids, but no. We're on our own for now," she said. It was like the air was sucked from the room. Despite what my father had done to us he was still our father and we loved him. We all knew we were going to miss him but we understood why he couldn't come with us.

My mother had one week to scrape up enough money to get us back to New York. She asked family members for help, but nobody was in a position to do so. When the seven days were up, she didn't have enough money to get us back home. The landlord came to our door and told us we had to be out by the next day. My mother started praying, asking for a way and asking God to lead the way. The only things we'd had when we arrived at that apartment was the clothes on our backs. Everything else had been given to us, so we packed our bags and left everything else behind, just like we'd done when we left New York to come to Florida. We all loaded up in the station wagon that night, homeless once again. Mom didn't have enough money to travel and was unsure if her car would even make it all the way back to New York, so she decided to sell it to buy us all one-way bus tickets back to New York. We were able to stay with my grandmother and uncles for the weekend while my mother went to sell her car, as well as some food stamps, to help pay for the trip back to New York for all seven of us.

And so that Sunday morning we grabbed our bags and headed to the bus station. Unfortunately, we had to leave some clothes behind since it was just my mother traveling with all six of us, all trying to juggle our belongings, but we were all looking forward to the next chapter in our lives. Hearing our bus announced over the intercom, we all grabbed our bags, my mother got us all settled together in our seats and off we went to New York.

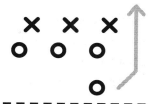

Back to Hudson

That trip north was rough for us all, especially for Mom, as she had all of her own things, some of our belongings, and our baby sister to carry around. Her attempts to sleep on the bus were futile, the conditions less than ideal as it was not only pretty uncomfortable but we also had to change buses five times. After a day and a half of travel we made it back to New York. We had to change buses in New York City but we had a layover for a few hours. This was actually my first time to NYC that I could remember. There was so many people in the bus station walking around, seemingly moving very fast in my young eyes. I loved watching all the different people move about the bus station, especially after having spent so many long hours on the bus. I took notice of a man maybe thirty feet away from us, yelling really loudly, shouting and swearing at everyone he walked by, and before I knew what was happening he was walking toward us. My mother spotted him and signaled for us to move in closer to her. The man was fast approaching and still shouting at people, calling them names for no reason. The man came near our area, stopped, and kept shouting, saying he hated everybody. My mother pulled us closer and the man looked at my mother and started directing insults at her, ranting on about how much he hated her and calling her names that I'm not even going to repeat. My brother and I were nervous, and as scared as we were, we stood up and puffed out our chests. We balled up our fists and told the man to leave our mother alone.

Another man standing by heard the commotion and saw what the shouting guy was doing and told him to get away from us and leave us alone. The crazy man walked away and out of the building while my siblings and I quickly hugged Mom and asked her if she was okay. As if things weren't stressful enough, we knew she didn't need this too. She said she was fine as long as we were. I couldn't believe what had happened. This was my first big taste of the craziness of the city and I was just glad somebody stepped in and helped us. This was definitely a time I wished my dad had been there. If Dad had been with us that guy would never have stopped in our area and he surely wouldn't have insulted my mother, I can assure you of that.

It was time to get back on the bus to make one more stop, in Albany. After a few hours' ride, my aunts and cousins were there to meet us at the Albany bus station, and they took us to their house in Hudson for the time being. It was December, just a few cold days away from Christmas, and while there was snow on the ground, we were glad to be back up north. We may have been homeless but we were in a place where we felt loved and welcome. It was easier for my mother to get a job back in New York than it had been in Florida, so I knew we wouldn't be without a home for long. Mom had had a decent job before we took off to Florida and she was hoping to get her position there back from her old employer.

My mother planned to get us a new place of our own right after the holidays. She wanted to use what money she had left to give us a nice Christmas first, and she worked hard because she wanted us to wake up on Christmas morning and be able to open presents that came from her, not just from other relatives.

Mom got her old job back and found us an apartment about a block from our old place. We were soon signed back into our old school and back to our previous routines. I had really missed Hudson when we left and was glad to be back for the second half of seventh grade at Hudson Middle School. Track and field season was coming up for me, so I signed up for that. Everything was going well and I was very pleased with how things were looking for me and my family. Still, my father was in Florida and we weren't sure when he was joining us in Hudson, but my mother assured us that she was sure he'd be back. We all really missed him.

○ ○ ○

That school year ended, and it was time for me to train for football season. I was now going to play for the JV team because the eighth grade was transferring to the high school. I was so happy to think I'd be playing high school football. I wasn't yet a freshman, but I was excited to play with the older, more experienced guys. I worked really hard all summer long, running up and down the street, and up and down the hills. I worked out as much as I could and always by myself; nobody would ever run or work out with me, I was almost always alone when I trained. I always had this burning desire to get better and prove myself—I guess it was a habit I developed when I wasn't able to walk. I always felt like I was playing from behind and always had to prove something to both myself and others.

Now getting ready to play ball with the "bigger guys" I was surprised to find out there was no weight requirement to play, since back in my Pop Warner days we had to be a certain weight or age. After finding that out, I ran a few more hills and lifted a few more weights, believing some extra bulk in the way of some lean muscle could help make me stronger and faster. I was all signed up for football and felt physically ready to play. We started practice in the heat of August and practice ran twice a day. I was proud of myself for having trained like I had because there were guys dropping like flies and throwing up while I was feeling good—still a little nervous, but ready. I knew my summer training had paid off when I saw the coaches take notice and everyone around me clenching their sides or throwing up, and I was running circles around them all with nothing more than a bit of heavy breathing at times. Committing myself to that hard summer exercise had really paid off.

In the first football game of that season, the coach let me start over some of the freshmen and sophomores. I wasn't a starter yet but the coaches were really impressed with what they saw in me. I had a very good first game, playing both a little running back and wide receiver. I also played special teams where I almost broke it for a touchdown. It was a lot of fun and any jitters I'd had were gone; I actually felt like I belonged there.

That season was going great and I was getting a decent amount of playing time, but one game in particular changed it for me. Coach had put me in at running back and they called a toss sweep play to me. The quarterback tossed me the ball. I ran to the sideline and cut it up the field so hard I broke about five tackles before I broke loose and ran for a seventy-yard touchdown. I was jumping for joy—it was my first touchdown on JV, and what a touchdown it was! The coaches were generous with their praise, telling me they really like the way I ran the ball, and they said it was clear that I ran with so much passion and purpose. Those words stuck with me the remainder of that season and reminded me of my purpose out on the field: I was there to receive a D1 scholarship and go to the NFL. That was my ultimate goal. I reminded myself that I'd worked too hard to get where I was to ever lose sight of my purpose again. I knew I ran with the passion I did because it was just years before that I'd been unable to even walk at all. I had trained my body to walk again, and having done that, I knew there was nothing I couldn't do if I set my mind to it. I knew that God gave me this wonderful gift to walk again and to breathe again and run faster than every kid I faced on the football field. I vowed to thank Him every time I scored a touchdown by dropping to one knee in the end zone.

It was an early lesson in my football career: if you work hard and train to get better, you'll be better. I never let anyone tell me I couldn't do something and I never believed something was impossible. I never just sat back. I accepted that I would work hard at anything I did, and I'd do whatever it took to find a way to succeed. I stopped putting limitations on things after I truly realized what I'd already accomplished at my young age.

○ ○ ○

My eighth-grade year was coming to an end and I'd scored a few touchdowns and showed great promise to be a starter for the next football season. The coaches told me, "Keep working hard, never be satisfied, and you'll go far in football."

Around that same time my father did return to Hudson after a long stay in Florida. He came back into our lives and it seemed like things were going well. He told me he had heard about how well I was doing in football and he was upset that he missed it but promised he wouldn't miss another game.

o o o

Over that summer, my uncle was at my house almost every morning to oversee my workout. He was one of those people that really believed in me, and he had been a football player himself. He was a linebacker and he'd always say he knew a good running back when he saw one. And we both knew I was a good running back. His confidence in me really kept me motivated and believing in myself. If it weren't for my uncle, I probably would not have been playing ball at all. When I played offensive lineman, he would always tell the coach to let me run the ball or play receiver because he knew how fast I was. He was very happy I'd had an awesome first year of JV football.

o o o

I was now a freshmen in high school and going into my second year of JV, projected as a starter. I was so proud of myself; I couldn't believe how far I'd come in such a short time. The ones who remembered my accident were surprised and happy for me because nobody saw what was coming next, not even me. There was little visual proof of my accident; the physical scars were all that now remained. I'd limped around for eighteen long months but through hard work and a gift from God, my ability to walk was fully restored. I'd held onto my NFL dream for many years and that dream still burned bright. While my condition may not have been ideal, it didn't stop me from dreaming.

The season started, and I had to compete with another guy for the starting job at running back. I knew I had to work harder than the other guy to be the starter but I didn't mind the competition—I was ready for anything.

We were competing every day in practice. I thought I won the starting job for sure, but the coaches ended up making us both starters. It was believed we were evenly matched and they didn't want to just give one of us the full-time job, so we split time at the first game of the season. The coach put me in to start the game, but I didn't run the ball. I ran out on a couple of dummy routes and I didn't get a chance to run the ball before coming out and letting the other running back in. The other guy was doing a very good job running the ball as I was standing on the sideline waiting for my chance to get back in the game. The coach called me over to go back in; he wanted me close to him for when he was ready to put me, and believe me, I was right there eagerly waiting. Coach gave the quarterback the next play and the team got in the huddle. I just wanted this play to be over fast so I could get in. I stood next to the coach and watched the quarterback toss the ball to the running back. He caught the pass and ran down the sideline, stiff-armed a defender, and ran for a touchdown. I was happy for him, and for our team, but I was also upset because I had to wait longer to get in because we were going on defense. We all cheered because it was our first touchdown of the year and we were already in the lead. As the second half came around I thought I would start the game but the coach put the other running back in while I was on the sideline watching again—I didn't get the chance to run the ball at all the first half so I thought I'd start the second half and get a chance to actually run.

The coach put me in at receiver and I ran a few routes and caught one pass. I almost broke the tackle but was wrestled down by a defender. The coach kept me in as receiver and they called a running play. The running back ran the ball up the middle, I ran and blocked the DB. The running back cut behind me and ran for his second touchdown. We had still been in the lead, but only by a point, so that touchdown put us over the top. Everyone was so happy and cheered for him and told me "Great block!" I was happy about what I'd done but I really wanted to run the ball. I went to the coach to find out when I could start really doing what I knew I did best.

"Coach, when do you think I can get in to run the ball?"

"What do you mean, Collins? I thought you did run the ball . . . Didn't you?" He scratched his head.

"No, Coach, not yet, but I'm ready," I said enthusiastically.

"Okay, get back in the line-up and I'll try to get you in on the next series."

I was so nervous when I heard that because although I wanted to run, I also wanted to match up to the other running back who had now already scored not just one, but two touchdowns. As far as I was concerned, I had things to prove both to my coach and to myself.

The other team had now scored, and they were kicking the ball off to us. The coach called the other running back in and he gave me a shout. "Collins! Stand by! You're going in on the next play!" he shouted down the sideline.

That was exactly what I'd wanted to hear, but I couldn't help being a little concerned that the other running back would score before I got the chance to get in. We were losing by six points with just a quarter and a half left in the game. I was just shocked that I hadn't had a chance to run the ball yet. Every time I thought my chance was coming around, it seemed like something happened, like a turnover or a touchdown. I played a lot of the game, just not as running back, which was where I really wanted to be. I thought I'd impressed the coaches enough to give me a good share of running back carries. I meant no disrespect to the other running back. He'd done very well, but I wanted my chance to show them what I was made of too.

By the start of the fourth quarter, I'd gone from knowing I was going to start at the beginning of the game, to now hoping I'd just get even a chance to carry the ball once. We were ahead, and it just so happened that the coach was putting me in at running back. I had my mind set that if they gave me a chance to run the ball I would absolutely capitalize on that opportunity. I told myself nothing was going to stop me if I got the chance. The coach called a running play as I stood in the huddle, heart beating faster than ever, hands shaking, and eyes wide open. I felt an anticipation that allowed me to only focus on scoring and not being stopped. We broke the huddle and walked to the line of scrimmage. Everything around me went silent except the quarterback's voice. The quarterback said down and then everything around me disappeared except the ball. The quarterback yelled hike, and I ran the counter play, stepping left and then going right as I got the ball, planted my feet in the fresh-cut grass, and ran fifty-five yards for my first touchdown of the year.

I could see that running play before I ran it.

I saw the touchdown before I ran it.

I couldn't believe I'd scored on my very first carry of the game. And I learned something on that carry—If I could create a movie in my mind, visualizing myself scoring a touchdown before the play, I had a better chance at a successful run. I decided that was something I was going to try every game. We ended up winning that day and I was pleased with the way I'd ended the game, although I still wanted to know why I hadn't had a chance to run the ball until the fourth quarter. The coach later explained to me that he went with "the hot hand." The other running back had been doing so well and the coach didn't want to curb his momentum. I understood that but I wasn't shy about pointing out that I didn't get to carry the ball until the fourth quarter and I had scored a fifty-five-yard touchdown myself. He said he thought I'd carried the ball in the first quarter, but he had been mistaken. He said he'd pay closer attention and he went on to congratulate me on my run.

The next week I got more chances to run the ball than I'd had the week before. I went on to have a successful rest of my freshman year, averaging over one hundred yards a game and two or three touchdowns.

Toward the end of the season I took over and became the full-time running back, as the other running back got injured. I took over the starting job and never slowed down. I was scoring touchdowns from anywhere on the field. When the other running back was ready to come back, it was decided that I was doing so well that the coaches didn't want to take me out. I exceeded even my own expectations that season. I had played an important part in my team winning games and competing to the end. I really felt proud to be a real part of the team.

High School

I was becoming well-known around Hudson as a very good football player. I certainly wasn't yet as big as some of the stars on the varsity team, but I was making enough of a name for myself where people were starting to recognize my ability. I had completed my second year of JV football and now it was time to really focus on schoolwork since I now had eyes on me. People wanted to be around me, something that was new for me, and that felt weird. I'd always had plenty of friends but suddenly my newfound athletic status made this all very different. People seemed to just want to be around me; just in my vicinity to hear about whatever I had going on. I was becoming somewhat of a celebrity, which was nothing I ever thought would happen this soon in my life or in my fledgling football career, but here I was, and it was happening.

There was only one problem to this new chapter in my life— Football was going so well I really felt I'd conquered a huge hurdle as I'd gone from not walking to now scoring touchdowns at will on the football field. But I was not happy with where I was in school. Much to my dismay, I was placed in a special education class because I was labeled as having a learning disability. I was so embarrassed with where I was in my academics and I dreaded going to school for fear of the other kids finding out I had challenges when it came to schoolwork despite being a good football player. I didn't feel like a real student as everyone went off to class when the bell rang and I had to do what I felt was a walk of shame to special ed. I really didn't want anybody to know, for fear I would be made fun of. I would always hear students making fun of those that were in special ed, or even in general ed classes . . . or just because a kid was different for that matter. I'd had to deal with a lot of being made fun of when I was crippled and I didn't want to go through that again, so I kept things pertaining to the classroom a secret for as long as I could. I even went so far as to take special precautions to make sure no one found out: I literally ran to my classroom when no one was around. I was late for class almost every day because I wouldn't go in the classroom until the last bell after the halls had cleared and everyone else was settled in class and out of the hallways. Special ed consisted of eight to ten students and three teachers and was designed for students who didn't learn as quickly as others; those who needed a little extra help. I guess I had always been in a slower-paced class and just hadn't really noticed it until people started noticing me. I asked my teacher why I was in a special class and I questioned her as to whether I'd ever get to go to a bigger, mainstream classroom.

"I certainly think that may be a future option for you," she said, "but we need to get you up to speed. Remember the last round of testing you went through? Unfortunately, your placement scores tell us that, for now, this class is the best fit for you."

Ever since my accident I had been a bit slower to learn new things when it came to academics, to the point that I was labeled as having a learning disability. I was aware I had had trouble learning new things and I had a major problem when it came to reading, whether it was just reading to myself, or out loud. I wasn't horrible at math, but I wasn't strong in that subject either. And to top it all off, I also had a hard time when it came to taking tests. I couldn't imagine ever remembering everything I was taught and when it was test time I froze up and seemed to forget even the things I thought I had remembered; it would all just be gone from my mind.

That was a very low time for me. It wasn't like I was pretending to be something I was not. I really didn't know who I was or who I should be. I knew I needed something different but didn't know what it was. My days in school consisted of me being in the same classroom all day, never getting the experience of switching classes and teachers and seeing new faces, aside from lunch and gym class. Lunch time was weird for me. It felt like I was always running into new kids that I'd never seen before, even though we shared the same school all along.

When I did see my friends at lunchtime, they routinely asked me where I'd been all day because they never saw me. I was too embarrassed to tell them I was in a special class for a learning disability, so the only way I knew to respond was by avoiding the question or changing the subject. Luckily for me, my classroom was near the back of the school under the stairs, without any other classroom nearby so it made it easy for me to slip in and out unnoticed. Because I always waited until the last minute to get to class and was late nearly every day, it did however, became a problem with my teacher.

"Leroy, I don't know where you are every day that causes you to be late," she said, "but I want you here on time before the second bell with no excuses. Do I make myself clear?" I shook my head, not wanting to divulge my fear of being found-out by my peers. "Your tardiness is getting in the way of your studies, as well as everyone else's when we have to delay the start of class while we wait for you every day. I'd hate to do it, Leroy, but I'm going to have to write you up if you arrive late one more time."

Obviously, I really didn't *want* to come in late, and I wanted to tell her my reasoning, but I was too ashamed to tell her the truth, and I certainly didn't want to hurt anyone else's feelings. I felt out of place there, as if I belonged someplace else; someplace where I could be challenged and experience new things. I believed I had more to offer and deep down I knew I wasn't tapping into my full potential.

○ ○ ○

One day I went home and told my mother I wanted to move to mainstream classes with the rest of my classmates.

"Please, Mom. I don't feel like I'm learning anything new and it's embarrassing to have to go into that classroom. If word gets out, they're gonna make fun of me, Mom. Do you really want that? I don't!" I implored her to get me out of special ed and she relented.

"Okay, okay . . . I hear what you're saying," she said. "Don't get too excited, but I'll call the school and see what we have to do to get you in some general classes. I can't make any promises, but for you, I'll try, baby." And as she promised, my mother made arrangements to talk to my guidance counselor.

"Mrs. Collins, I'm sorry that it isn't as easy as simply submitting a request; it doesn't work that way. Leroy will have to be tested in order to be placed and even then, each teacher would have to agree to accept him midyear."

"Whatever you have to do," my mother said, "I just want him switched."

"I understand the situation may be less than ideal from Leroy's perspective, but I have to say, I personally don't think it would be a good idea for Leroy to leave the special ed setting since the class does provide the help he needs. I can't help but think he'd feel significantly challenged if he was to transfer to mainstream classes at this stage of the game. I'm afraid he'll never make it. He's just too far behind and I can't see him being able to keep up with the work. They teach an aggressive curriculum and they do move through the material pretty fast."

My mother politely disagreed and reiterated that she wanted me moved out of special ed. It was not long after that that the school administration met and agreed to move me. As I signed out, the guidance counselor had a few parting words for me: "Now you'll never graduate and you'll never go to college." Those words, coming from someone in such a position, someone meant to guide and encourage young people, stuck with me for a long time and fueled my fire whenever things got tough. From that moment, I was determined to not only prove that woman wrong, but I also made a point of remembering all those who counted me out before I even got started.

o o o

I was moved and started my first day in general classes with the rest of my classmates. I knew most of the kids in my new setting and was introduced to the ones that I'd always seen around school but didn't know well. I knew my pessimistic guidance counselor was wrong for what she said, but she was right about the class moving fast. I was like a deer in headlights as the lessons were coming fast. It was admittedly hard for me to keep up and I felt like I wasn't understanding a thing. I was shocked to see how far behind I'd already fallen in a short period of time and I felt so small in that class. I was truly in a different world.

I think for the first few days I sat in all my different classes just praying that the teachers didn't call on me. I couldn't help but hear the guidance counselor's words echo in the back of my mind, but rather than allow those words to knock me down, I asked for extra help because I had to admit I was lost and I knew I needed to somehow keep my head above water. Going to my teachers and asking for help, I also asked them to please not say anything to my guidance counselor. I was too worried that she'd immediately want to send me back to special ed and I wasn't about to just throw in the towel.

One day I had no choice but to voice my concerns to my mother.

"Roy! You know you need to come out here and have some breakfast before you head off to school," she called. "C'mon, baby . . . you're gonna be late!"

I reluctantly emerged from my room and dragged myself down the hall, feeling the weight of my worries. "Mom, I'm a little afraid to go to school . . ."

"Well now, why would you say that? We got you in those regular classes, just like you wanted," she reminded me.

"Because I don't know anything, not the stuff the other kids do." I hesitated to go on but she was staring at me expectantly, waiting for a further explanation. "The classes are a bit harder than I thought they'd be," I admitted.

"So, what do you think we should do about that? If you want to remain in those classes with your friends then we're just going to have to dig a little deeper." I could see her thinking as she continued to get breakfast on the table. "I'll help you with your homework and to study for tests, and let's see about your teachers helping you after school or during lunch."

From that day on, Mom and I established a routine where she stuck to her end of the deal and I gladly accepted the help. We studied together every day, even on Sundays, until I started to better understand the work that was being taught in class. My mother and I were both determined to prove that guidance counselor wrong. I know it broke Mom's heart to think somebody felt that way about her son and she continued to feel a certain amount of guilt for the truck accident those years ago that she believed was now affecting my abilities. She always wanted to give me and the rest of the kids the best possible chance to succeed, even if that meant she came home from work exhausted, cooked for all of us, and then spent hours giving us the support and encouragement we needed with our schoolwork.

As I worked to catch up, it proved to be a hard journey. When we received our report cards at the end of that year, I saw it there on paper, spelled out clearly for the first time. I hadn't done so well: a few Cs, Ds, and Fs. I was devastated. Feeling disappointed in myself, I thought I'd also let my mother down and I cringed at the thought of my guidance counselor sitting in her office smiling with satisfaction.

As I entered the guidance office one afternoon to get information about summer school, I was feeling the weight of the world on my shoulders and my stomach dropped when I saw my counselor give me a knowing glance. She looked at me as if to say, "See? I told you so . . ." I walked out of that office feeling like I wasn't prepared to even attend the remedial summer school classes. I wasn't sure what I was going to do, but I knew I needed to do well if I wanted to play football in the fall, so failing was not an option. I believed, at the time, I was more nervous about never understanding my schoolwork rather than if I'd be able to play football; and I had this shadow of doubt that drove me to focus on nothing but being unsuccessful in school rather than focusing on recalling all the hills I'd already climbed in my life.

Summer school that year ended up not being hard at all. The teachers there really helped me and focused on everyone in the class succeeding. It was nothing like our regular school work. I was actually glad I went because it changed my approach to my education.

That summer, one of the teachers in particular gave me additional help after I told her what I'd been struggling with. She helped me get over the anxiety I'd been experiencing when I had to read something aloud. "What you're feeling isn't that unusual," she said. "There are a lot of people who fear subjects just based on a lack of understanding, and I'm not just talking about students. I know plenty of adults who fear things they know nothing about. That's why they say knowledge is power. If you're afraid of what you don't know, you start to forget the things you do know."

Applying this new way of thinking to my own situation changed the way I studied and my general outlook on education. I made up my mind that I was not going to be afraid anymore, and I learned new things every day without even focusing on them. I then felt more confident going to school because I chose not to be afraid of learning things I knew nothing about. As time went on I really made huge strides academically.

○ ○ ○

I was now a sophomore and it was football season once again. I thought I was going to be playing JV another year because the varsity team had two returning seniors at running back and the guy I'd competed with the previous year was a sophomore. But the coaches had other plans for me. They wanted me on the varsity team to be a relief guy for the two seniors. I had mixed feelings about this switch because I liked the idea of staying on JV, which would allow me to be the starter and rack up a lot of points and yardage. I really didn't want to play on varsity just to sit on the bench, hoping for time on the field. But I went anyway.

The coaches put me at third-string running back and I was the starting kick-off return and punt return guy. I had no idea how that season was going to go or what to expect but I showed up every day ready to practice and trying to contain my eagerness to move up the roster. The starting senior was very good and while I didn't think I'd take his spot, nothing was going to stop me from trying. I was confident I could outplay the second-string guy though. He wasn't as good as the starter and I knew I'd just need a chance to run the ball and show them what I could do. I had worked hard the entire off-season and I needed to be in the game if I was ever going to achieve my dream of going to the NFL. I went all out in practice, even if that upset my teammates at times. I gave it everything I had, every chance I had.

○ ○ ○

As we got a few games under our belts, the season was going well and I was playing a little more than I thought I would. I scored a few touchdowns and rushed for over five hundred yards. I did well enough for the coaches to tell me I was going to be their starter next season and they were going to win a championship with me in the backfield. Boy, how times had changed! I was doing enough so that everyone around me was now a believer.

○ ○ ○

Football was going great, but I was still struggling with school. I was focused but it was coming at me fast. I was being tutored and my mother still helped when she could, which gave me an advantage. My grades were a little better than they'd been in the past, but I did work slower than other students. My sophomore year was coming to a close. I hadn't done as well as I'd wanted to, but I did much better than I'd done the year before, so that was progress.

I attended summer school for my second year in a row. Feeling more confident in class made me happy as I passed and was officially a junior.

The coaches told me I was going to be the starter, so I worked very hard on that off-season. I wanted to do something that had never been done in Hudson football. I wanted to break the rushing record and I wanted to win a championship.

More on My Plate

The new school year started, and I couldn't wait to be the starting running back for the varsity football team. Everybody knew it and anticipated watching me play. I walked into school on a Friday, the day of our first game of the year, and my guidance counselor pulled me into her office, letting me know I didn't have enough credits to meet the graduation requirements. Even if I passed everything from both junior and senior year, I wouldn't have enough to graduate. I asked her what I could do, because I obviously needed to graduate. "There must be something I can do . . . ?" She told me there wasn't. I called my mother and she told me not to worry; she was going to figure something out.

I put my focus back on the game we had that night. It would be my first game as a starter for varsity, and I'd heard the whole town would be there to see me run the ball. It was game time—Friday night lights—my favorite day of the week.

As the bus pulled up to the sports complex, I looked out the window and saw a stadium full of people. My stomach dropped. I closed my eyes and prayed the 121 Psalm. "I lift up mine eyes unto the hills, from whence cometh my help. My help cometh from the Lord which made Heaven and Earth. He will not suffer thy foot to be moved: he that keepeth thee will not slumber. Behold, he that keepeth Israel shall neither slumber nor sleep. The Lord is thy keeper: The Lord is thy shade upon thy right hand. The sun shall not smite thee by day, nor the moon by night. The Lord shall preserve thee from evil: He shall preserve thy soul. The Lord shall preserve thy going out and coming in from this time forth and even for evermore, Amen." Since my freshman year of football, that prayer had always calmed my nerves, giving me a sense of peace but letting me know I was ready for war. Until now I'd only said it privately to myself, but I decided that, for this game, I was going to say it aloud for my team and coaches. After we warmed up, I gathered the team before the National Anthem. I asked them all to take a knee and grab someone's hand, as I recited Psalms 121.

The team was energized and ready to play. At the start of the game I ran out there on kick-off return. The other team kicked off. My teammate caught the ball and took off down the field, tackled only after gaining many yards. I stayed on the field to line up at the running back position. I was so happy to know I had all my family there. Everybody came out to watch us play. It was like the city shut down for Friday night football. First play of the game was a running play to me. I picked up decent yards as I started to see the pictures in my head as to what I could've done to change that play. We got into the huddle call for the next play. It was a play to the fullback up the middle, so I faked as if I was getting a toss sweep and the quarterback gave the ball to the fullback and then pretended to throw me the ball. The fullback almost broke it.

We headed back to the huddle and the quarterback called a toss sweep to me. I started to see the picture in my mind: I envisioned myself scoring a touchdown on this play. We broke the huddle and as I walked to the line of scrimmage, my focus increased. I listened to the cadence, the quarterback yelled "Hike!" I ran, extending my arm to receive the ball. When I caught the ball, I noticed there was a guy running right for me. I saw the cutback just like I'd envisioned before we broke the huddle. I planted my foot as I turned my head and shoulders to the cutback area. As I made a move, I avoided the defender but as I was running by him he grabbed my face mask, pulled on it to bring me down. I heard a *pop*, my feet flew up, I landed on my back and as my head smashed to the ground everything went black. I lay on the ground, unresponsive, everybody around me shaking me in an attempt to wake me up. The coaches and ambulance immediately responded, instructing no one move me. My mother and father rushed to me in a panic; my mother already praying. Both teams had taken a knee as the world paused. I opened my eyes to the EMTs putting me on a stretcher. "Can you feel your feet?" they asked. They also asked me to squeeze their hand. After a brief assessment, they loaded me into the ambulance and I gave the crowd a thumbs-up. I could hear them chanting, "Leroy! Leroy!" and that felt so good to hear.

On my way to the hospital I broke down in tears. This was not the way I'd wanted things to go. It was our first game of the season and I was in an ambulance on my way to the hospital. I was also bothered by the news I'd received earlier in the day about not having enough credits for graduation. Boy, oh boy, my day was just not going well. When I reached the hospital all I wanted to do was head back to the football field to finish the game. I pleaded with the doctor to be permitted to go back and play but he told me I wouldn't be playing any more football that night whereas they'd have to run tests and rule out any broken bones. Tests were run, and I was fine. I told him I'd heard a pop before I blacked out, but the doctor said there was no sign of anything wrong. A few hours passed before I was released, and the coaches and my teammates came to the hospital to see me.

I was released with no restrictions. Luckily, I was still able to practice and play in the game scheduled for the next weekend. My parents had been thanking God and praying the entire time. My mother said, "You have to thank God even when things are bad and don't look right." I felt a bit guilty that day. My mother hadn't wanted me to play football in the first place, yet now she was sitting with me in the hospital. After evaluating me, the doctor said everything was fine and I was able to return to football. But he also said something that scared my mother, really bringing all the guilt right back to her. He said if I had broken my neck I could've been paralyzed, or even worse, died. My mother didn't need to hear that. She had already experienced both of those fears once and really did not want to relive them.

We left the hospital late and all I wanted to do was rest, so when I got home I went straight to bed. Before I went to sleep that night, I started reflecting. I had wanted that day to go so well but it began with horrible news and ended in the hospital. At that point I just wanted that day to end and to be able to hit the reset button. I was lying down but it was hard to fall to sleep as I was feeling uncomfortably sore. My mind raced thinking about the game and thinking about how it could've all been over in a flash. I finally fell asleep after lying there for a few hours and I woke up with an incredibly sore neck—I could barely move. I definitely felt as if something was wrong, but I remembered the doctor saying I was fine and could return to playing ball that following week. My mother called the doctor anyway as a precaution and told him how I was feeling. He just instructed me to rest for the weekend and to call his office if I was still in pain on Monday.

My body clearly knew it needed rest and it forced me to do so because I truly couldn't move without pain. Monday rolled around and I was still a little sore, but nothing like Saturday morning. I decided we didn't need to call the doctor because the pain was going away and I didn't want there to be a chance of being told I couldn't play.

By Wednesday of that week I was feeling better still, and ready to play in our next game. I was having an amazing junior year in football and I was even catching up with my school work. I was still bothered by the fact that I wouldn't graduate on time no matter how well I did now. I'd done so poorly back in my freshman and sophomore years, that it just wasn't enough, and I'd have to come to terms with this reality.

My mother found a program that helped students who were short on graduation credits. It was actually an extra credit correspondence course through the college. I'd missed the summer session, so I had to wait until Christmas break to start, but the weekly program also had classes during winter break, spring break, and summer. I needed all those classes if I wanted to graduate on time. Whatever it took, I was willing to do it to be sure my counselor's prediction didn't come true. The courses were expensive and we didn't really have the money, but my parents had time to come up with a plan to save for it.

○ ○ ○

Football was exceeding my expectations. The year had started out a little scary, but I'd bounced back strong and determined. I rushed for over one thousand yards and twenty-eight touchdowns. My team was also in the Buckley Cup game with a conference rivalry cup kept by the winning school. We took the Cup home with us my junior year and we also made it to sectionals (but lost in the first round). The team we played in the first round of sectionals really had our number—they keyed in on me the whole game, their plan to stop me in particular was obvious, and they'd succeeded. That was the only team all year who had stopped me from scoring and kept me under one hundred yards. In all my time playing running back I'd never felt so contained. It was like the other team knew where I was going to be and what I was going to do. As soon as I touched the ball they were all over me. I was getting very frustrated and was nearly ejected from the game. One of our players fumbled the ball and I went to get it. A player decided to earhole me instead of going after the ball. I was angry because that really rung my bell and left me seeing double. I got up off the ground and threw a punch at the closest person, but I missed him and ended up falling again. I was unsure as to who had hit me, and I was dazed, figuring it had to be the person closest to me. While the ref sent me to the sideline to calm down, at least he didn't eject me, so that was something to be thankful for because, really, I would have deserved it under other circumstances.

That was a tough loss, but I learned something that day—I think it needed to happen. I had been doing so well I'd forgotten about my craft, my blessing, and my team. When things were going well I took most of the credit and when things were going poorly I was quick to point a finger. I wasn't raised that way and my mother would've been disappointed in me if she'd known. I hated to lose but I was glad it happened when it did. It brought me back to reality. I still had my hopes and dreams of making it to the NFL, and at times, that was all I thought about. The idea of my team helping me get there wasn't part of my plan and yet it should've been at the top of my list. I refocused on my plan and took care to include my teammates and coaches. I also thought long and hard about how that opposing team had stopped me from performing my best. In the game film it was easy to see that they'd flowed with me—wherever I stepped they stepped. They tackled me when I didn't even have the ball.

I decided I'd have to change my style of running and learn how to read defense to give myself an advantage when the team was keying on me. Ninety percent of my runs were on the outside; I used the cutback every chance I had. I had to learn how to run up the middle with precision. I couldn't wait to train and practice it, and I made sure to let my teammates know what my plans were as far as working out and training for the upcoming season.

o o o

By the first week of December it was time for me to sign up for the correspondence courses for graduation. My mother contacted the high school and told them I was enrolling, and that the college would need my transcript. My roadmap to graduation allowed for no Christmas break, no winter break, and no summer break for the next two years—I was going to school year-round. Each course would cost $800, which we didn't have. Neither my mother nor I knew where that money would come from. We just operated on faith and believed everything was going to work out.

I wanted to do well in these new courses and not let my mother down. She sacrificed a lot for me to take these classes and if I failed I would be letting us both down. School let out for Christmas break and I had to start my first course; a three-hour night class, Monday through Friday, for two weeks. My first night there I felt lost within the first hour; I had no idea what the teacher was talking about. I just sat there writing things down that I didn't understand, probably misspelling it as I went, I thought. I knew it wasn't doing me any good by sitting there pretending; I was just setting myself up for failure. Better to say something before I got myself too far behind and struggled to pass, I thought. (There were times when I didn't say anything and paid for it later.) I knew this couldn't be one of those times, so I spoke up and told the teacher I didn't understand, and a few other students raised their hands as well. The teacher seemed to understand our struggles and reviewed the material again. She didn't want any of us to fail because she knew this was a last resort for most of us. She taught the lesson a little slower but fast enough that we finished on time, learning about computers, their keys and functions. Much of the class was taught on the chalkboard because the classroom only had two computers. Computer was fairly new back then and were hard to come by. We had to start learning them because they would soon be in every classroom. The teacher was throwing a lot of information at us in preparation for the final exam in just two weeks. Learning about something that was new to the world was good but very challenging. I was mentally exhausted. On test day, I was nervous but believed I understood enough material to pass the class.

As I took the test it seemed the other students were running circles around me as they finished. I started to panic and began to rush as I wondered how they could be done so fast. Maybe I didn't understand as much as I thought I had. It wasn't long before I was the only student there still taking my test. I had one more question to answer. I was going to guess but I decided to slow down and give myself the best possible chance to pass.

o o o

I had to wait a few weeks to get my final grade, but I was glad I'd finished the course. Christmas break was over, and school was starting up again. Everyone was talking about how much fun they'd had, the trips they'd went on, and the gifts they'd received. The teacher was polling the class about the holidays and she asked me about mine. I was too embarrassed to tell her (and the rest of the class) that I had been in school during the holiday vacation in order to graduate on time. So instead I made up a story about something fun and hoped they believed it. Nobody knew I had to take classes to graduate except for my parents, my guidance counselor, and the principal.

I came home from school one day and my mother handed me a letter of congratulations on passing my first correspondence course. She said, "You did it, Roy! Your hard work paid off. This is just the beginning, baby. I know you can accomplish anything you put your mind to, and I know you believe that too."

My mother was right. I started to believe that nothing was impossible even if it had seemed impossible. I knew it wasn't; not after everything I'd overcome in my young life so far. My mother was so happy, and I started to gain confidence in my ability to learn. I went on to take the winter and spring courses; they were very tough, but I passed them both. My junior year in high school was going well and I was starting to receive letters from colleges that wanted me at their schools to play football. I felt like a superstar getting mail from places like Florida State, North Carolina, and bunch of other D1 schools. This was something I'd dreamed about so long ago, and now it was time for it all to come to life. Colleges even came to my high school just to see me walk by. I wasn't allowed to talk to them and they weren't allowed to approach me until sometime the following year, so I was amazed that they traveled so far just for a glimpse of me. Me!? The dream I'd had as a little boy unable to walk was so big that it was hard for anyone else to see. It seemed unreal—hard to believe and hard to describe even now all these years later. But I believed and never stopped fighting to get where I now found myself, with letters from D1 schools addressed to me—Leroy Collins. It made my vision clearer and brought my dream closer, opening the eyes of those who couldn't see it and opening the hearts of people who hadn't believed.

o o o

The school year was ending and I had my summertime correspondence courses starting up—something I wasn't ready for at all. I just wanted to get ready for football season; that required a lot of training and focus. I know I had to sacrifice school breaks if I wanted to graduate with my class, but it got so hard that I wanted to quit at times. I was happy with what I'd accomplished but I was feeling mentally worn. I wanted to be prepared for football season because I'd set the goal of breaking the school record, to a win championship, and to be one of the best running backs in the country.

I felt like going to the additional classes would get in the way of my focus and my time to train for football. It was something

I needed to do, but I sure didn't want to. Something then happened that changed my whole focus and reminded me of how things can change at a drop of a hat.

My brother, cousin, and I, along with a few friends, went to a club near Albany. I'd just gotten a new car, so I drove. There were six of us and my car only fit five, so it was an uncomfortable ride for those in the back seat. We arrived at the club safe and sound, and it was Under 21 Night so we were able to gain access. Everything was going great inside the club. I wasn't allowed to drink because I had an "Under 21" hand stamp, but I asked someone of age to get me a drink. Well, as you might be able to predict, I ended up having a few anyway.

As the night ended we were all outside the club talking to some people we'd met, and we heard a bunch of shouting and bottles being broken where a crowd had come together. My brother and I stayed back and didn't get too close to the action but it turned out the action decided to come to us by way of a guy who had run out of the crowd with another guy chasing him, headed in our direction. I pulled my brother back out of the way just in case we had to run. The men ran right by us and I pulled my brother back as we could clearly see that the second guy had a knife sticking out of his neck. The man running away was obviously the one who had stabbed him, there was no mistake about that. The victim never caught his attacker, but we saw him drop to the ground in the distance and in no time the police showed up, so we took off before we got trapped.

We all were tired when we got in the car and my cousin asked if he could drive. I assured him I felt okay and that I'd drive us back. We ended up stopping at a Dunkin' Donuts because I wasn't feeling okay after all. I was exhausted and needed coffee in a bad way. It was a forty-five-minute ride back to Hudson, it was late, and we were tired. I drank my coffee while driving and talking to the guys about what we'd witnessed outside the club. The conversation lasted about ten minutes, then the car grew silent so I turned the music on and tried to focus on the winding roads. About twenty minutes later, I woke up behind the wheel on a sharp turn heading toward a cliffside guardrail. My eyes flew open and I turned the car quick, just missing the edge of the cliff. I looked in the back seat . . . Everybody back there was asleep and my cousin was asleep in the front seat as well. I don't know when I nodded off; all I knew was that I'd been talking for the first ten minutes of the drive and now I was miraculously about ten minutes from home when I woke up. I couldn't believe I'd just driven twenty minutes or so, dead asleep, and woken up right before a crash. I rolled the windows down, turned the music up and started singing to stay awake. Everybody in the car woke up and thought I was crazy—no one believed my account about how we got back to Hudson that night.

I thanked Jesus because there was no way I could've done what I did on my own. I sat there in disbelief, trying to figure it all out. There was no explanation. I fell asleep and we drove over twenty-five miles with all of us asleep in the car. I know I didn't switch highways and I know I didn't take the exit. I know I didn't take those turns, so it had to be God who took control while we slept. Talk about "Jesus take the wheel!" Jesus took it and guided us safely. I was so grateful to be able to look back and see my guys in the back seat asleep, and my cousin next to me. I kept imagining all the lives I would've affected if we'd crashed. I kept seeing my brother and thinking of how my mother would feel. My heart hurt just thinking about it.

After "the incident" I began to take summer school a little more seriously. My opportunity (for everything life could ever offer) could've been over in a split second. I started appreciating

Leroy Collins
FEBRUARY 9, 2016

Post game interview

1994

the little things and I took nothing for granted. I went to summer school and I looked at the experience as a stepping stone to college rather than a punishment. With a fresh outlook on my education, I trained hard and prepared myself for the football season.

o o o

Football season was the best time of the year (and still is). I was excited the season was here, but I was also sad because I was now a senior and this would be my last year to play for the Blue Hawks. I wanted to give them my best; I'd laid it all on the line. We planned on winning the championship and I planned on being the best running back in the country. I went into my senior season a little stronger and a little faster than I had been the year before.

We were ready to make history and we had the city behind us. We started the season off right. Our first opponent was Rensselaer and we beat them 26–6. This team had a great running back named DJ. He ran really hard and was always one step away from breaking it for a touchdown. So I knew I had to have a great game to help us advance past this team. I ended the game with 217 yards on 16 carries, which I thought was a great start on my mission to break the New York State rushing record, and the win was one step closer to a championship. We knew we had to face this team again so we were happy to have one up on them. We celebrated over the weekend and it was back to work to focus on our second opponent, Mohonasen. We were amped up for this game and we felt another victory coming. The game started off slow and with lots of penalties; we would have to have a big gain and penalties to bring it back. As it ended up, I would make a long run for a touchdown and it would be called back. I would break another long one and that would be called back as well. Penalties were destroying us. We totaled 130 yards worth of penalties during that game—more negative yards then we had in positive yardage. That was a hard-fought game but we came out on top, defeating Mohonasen 17–0. I rushed for 103 yards on the day. It wasn't the day I was hoping to have, but we got the victory and we were another step closer to the championship. We knew we had to be better prepared for our next opponent. They were undefeated, like we were, and they scored more points on their opponents then we did. LaSalle was next on our schedule and they were considered one of the three top teams in the western division by most observers, and also by the way they manhandled powerhouse Albany Academy,

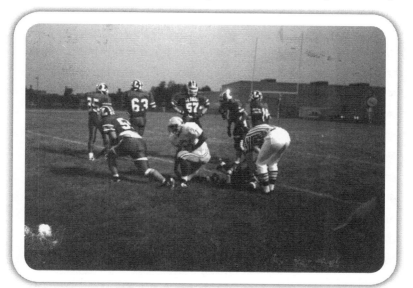

Surrounded by tacklers

1994

defeating them 34–0. We definitely had our work cut out for us. Our defense had to set their game up if we were going to survive this one. LaSalle had two speedsters in their backfield, Carter and Johnson, who routinely gave teams a hard time. The Blue Hawks were ready for the challenge.

The day of the game against LaSalle I felt really good about it and I dropped down on my knees and prayed, "Lord, give me strength and give us victory." I got up off my knees and was ready to play. It was game time as far as I was concerned, and from the first kick-off to the last play, we controlled the game. Our defense did an amazing job stopping LaSalle from scoring and shutting down two of the most feared running backs in Section 2. In the end, we were victorious, defeating LaSalle 27–0. I had over 200 yards and 2 touchdowns, which put me back on track to break the NYS rushing title. We subsequently went on to beat Ravena 37–6 and destroyed Schalmont 43–7. The season was going just the way we predicted. We were generating quite a buzz throughout New York State high school football. People were traveling from far and wide to see us play—we packed the stadiums every game. We had big write-ups in the paper every week and we made the news almost as often.

The team was stacked—we had one of the best field-goal kickers in the state, led by Lacasse, and one of the best defenses in the section. The defense was led by my younger brother, Ernest Collins, the very same brother who had nearly been killed that day in the accident on the street with me years before. He was a force to be reckoned with, in on or making almost every tackle. He was definitely a rising star and played both sides of the ball like it was his last chance. I was leading in almost every category as a running back and we had some excellent receivers. I would say we had a championship team but we had to get through a few opponents before we could celebrate and our next opponent was no slouch. Their record didn't show how dangerous they were. They weren't winning many games but they were coming close and wanted to knock us off our horse and hand us our first loss, so we couldn't take them lightly and look past them or underestimate them if we wanted to win. We ended up being victorious and defeating Albany Academy 31–7. I carried the ball 22 times and rushed for 180 yards, which was some hard-fought yards, as I recall. They were really laying some hits on me. I guessed they figured if they broke me down they had a better chance at winning. They must've forgotten we had a quarterback that could throw the ball and a fullback that could really run. We also had three receivers that could catch consistently, so then they keyed in on me. A hand off to our fullback or pass to our receiver had them on their heels so it made it easier later in the game for me to pick up yards. I was not really breaking a long run like I had been in prior games according to what was expected of me. I was getting a few yards here and a few yards there, moving the ball but definitely feeling the pressure. I just kept pounding away, knowing if I continued running hard they would eventually fold. And they did. The fourth quarter came around and the quarterback AJ Mueller handed me the ball up the middle. I was going to make a cut to the outside but the line opened up this gaping hole so I stayed straight and ran for a sixty-eight-yard touchdown with six minutes left in the game. It was an amazing night as we got the win, putting our record now at 6–0, and I'd personally rushed over one thousand yards, which got me closer to breaking the NYS rush record. We had a few games left and if I wanted to break the record I'd have to find a way to run a little harder or be more elusive and gain more yards from here on out.

I watched film on Averill Park, learning how their defense flowed and trying to find weaknesses so I could take advantage of them. This Averill Park game was also our homecoming game and there were a lot of activities leading up to days before the game and on game day. I was nominated to be Homecoming King, but really had no interest. My focus was on beating Averill Park and gaining as many yards as I could on game day in order to get me closer to the rushing record. It turned out that I was named Homecoming King and I wasn't looking forward to dealing with the homecoming halftime show and the coronation. I really didn't think I'd win what was basically a popularity contest, and

Homecoming King

1994

I wanted it to end as soon as possible so we could get back to the game. I was standing there with my Homecoming date and when my name was announced as king, I really didn't know what to do because I'd been thinking of nothing other than football. I did my best to just put on a quick happy face, eager to get the game going. I just wanted to play football—I was very serious about my goal to win a championship. But on a social level, I certainly didn't want to be rude to school tradition, so I went with it, all the while thinking that being crowned in the middle of a football game was not going to get us to a championship. In the end, we won that game, and every other game of the regular season, and it was off to sectionals.

We defeated Rensselaer for the second time that year and brought the Buckley Cup home to Hudson for the second year in a row. Our first round of sectional games was against Greenwich. They had a very good team and had a very explosive offense and a dynamic defense. We were ready for this team but cautious because we'd lost in the first round the previous year to Cambridge. So, we came together and refused to lose this year's sectional game. We went on to beat Greenwich 57–12 and I rushed for 162 yards and three touchdowns. Our record was then 10–0 and I rushed for 1,864 yards—getting closer to the New York State rushing record, and closer to a championship. That was an amazing time—we were an amazing team and we had amazing supporters. Away games were just like our home games—the city of Hudson would shut down when the Blue Hawks played. That was really a special season because we really had the chance to take Hudson football further than it had been in a very long time.

o o o

I broke the Section 2 rushing record and the touchdown record, and I was on my way to breaking the NYS rushing record. But that wasn't going to happen if we didn't make it past our next opponent, who had only allowed fifteen points to be scored on them all year. This was set to be my toughest game yet; I was facing a defense that had stopped everybody from scoring on them. I have to admit I was a little nervous as to why anyone wasn't scoring on this team—they were clearly *that* good. They seemed to be a step above the competition in their league and I had to wonder if I had what it took to perform better than their previous running back. We would soon see.

Leroy Collins famous V-8 move

1994

I ended that game with over 250 yards and two touchdowns—we won, defeating them 14–6. I'm not going to say it was an easy task to gain the yardage and score as many points as I had against a team that had such a strong defense, but our team played well and I had great blocks. (I will say I don't think they'd never met a running back like me before either.)

We were so excited we beat a team that everyone thought we would lose to. We were now 11–0, defeating everyone that challenged us and silencing all critics who were waiting for us to lose, not believing we were as good as we were proving to be week after week.

On to States

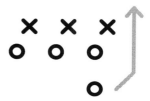

We had to play Nanuet, a tough team near New York City with the same record we had, and nearly the same scoring throughout the season. We were on a mission, no matter how tough they were or how fierce they sounded in the papers. We were tough too and no one we'd faced had come close to stopping us.

I had read about a Nanuet running back who was very good; he had all the tools—he was fast, powerful, and he knew how to score. Right before the big game, I ducked into the bathroom before the National Anthem and there stood the Nanuet star running back himself. He was with a few other players putting some eye black on. They seemed to recognize me right away. My Number 23 was all over the place, so they knew who I was. They'd probably heard stories about my running style or read some article about my success on the field. They probably thought they were going to see some giant based on the many stories they'd heard. But instead they saw this skinny kid with huge shoulder pads and walked out laughing. "He don't look so tough . . ." they said.

Just wait and see, I thought.

Nanuet got the first kick-off, we stopped them, and they kicked the ball off to us. In my very first carry of the game I took the ball down the sideline and ran fifty-four yards for a touchdown. The crowd went crazy and the Nanuet team stood in disbelief—they didn't know what hit them. They'd heard the stories about me and they'd scouted me on films, but they never believed that it could happen to them. I rushed over to the sideline, feeling the change in energy. I saw hope in the eyes of my teammates and I heard victory in their shouts. After the touchdown run the whole atmosphere changed; we felt in control. I was picking up some big yards, but it was mostly back and forth for the game up to less than ten minutes left in the fourth quarter. We were ahead 7–6 and they were driving the ball, big play after big play. The clock was ticking, and it seemed like they could score at any play, the way they were moving the ball. They caught a pass and were tackled at our eleven-yard line.

The stadium went quiet while the crowd watched Nanuet slice through our defense. The cheers turned to worry because if Nanuet scored a touchdown, they would take the lead without much time on the clock. They did a pop pass on a first down and gained five yards. The coach asked me to play defensive end for the next few plays. He said he needed speed to stop them behind the line of scrimmage. They ran the ball on second down and gained three yards. They needed two more yards for a first down or three yards for a touchdown, with six minutes left on the clock. They ran the ball again on third down and were stopped with a one-yard loss. It was fourth down. We thought they'd kick it but they took their chances and decided to go for it. I was still in as a defensive end and Nanuet lined up to run their play on fourth down after losing a yard.

They ran a running play. I pushed passed the offensive lineman and saw the running back get the ball from the quarterback. He tried to cut it back in and push his way to a first down or touchdown. I lunged at him and caught him in the air as soon as he tried to dive and I brought him down. We went down and all the players fell on top of each other. The refs called out the chain gang to see if they picked up a first down. The stadium was quiet and our hearts were beating fast as the ref proceeded with the measuring. He went down to measure and stood up with the "One inch too short" signal and said, "Hudson, first down!" The crowd went crazy. Players were jumping up and down, the spectators were falling out of their seats. We'd stopped them and now it was time to close the game out with a victory.

We had a few nice plays to get us down to the red zone and a few plays later I caught a toss sweep and ran down the sideline for a fifteen-yard scamper and jumped over a player right before I landed in the end zone for a touchdown. We were confident we'd win the game now. Nanuet had one more chance to tie the game up and send us into overtime. The running back I'd seen before the game was pretty quiet now. With three minutes left in the game he caught a pass up the middle and almost took it for a touchdown before he was stopped. They attempted to complete another pass play, but our Hawk defense intercepted the ball to close out the game.

We were ready and preparing to go to Syracuse to play in the Carrier Dome for the state championship. This was a dream come true. We had set our goal at the beginning of the year to make this a championship season, and here we were. We were shocked to be getting ready to play in a D1 stadium—the dream of every high school football player.

o o o

We got to Syracuse the day before our game, staying in a hotel around the corner from the stadium. We were treated like kings on this entire NYS championship journey. It was all definitely much more than any of us expected. We had a team meal, a team meeting, and then lights out. Well, kinda . . . We waited for the coaches to do a room check, then we all met up in one room. Some players brought alcohol and snacks, so we made some mixed drinks and ate. Some friends had traveled from Hudson and they brought more alcohol. We were wrestling and joking, and running up and down the halls until about 1:00 a.m. Our game was in just ten hours, so we decided to call it a night.

More than half our team woke up the next day hungover and not feeling well. Nobody wanted to get up, especially to eat breakfast and practice before the game. I knew I'd messed up as soon I opened my eyes—I felt like crap. I had been so focused and ready to put on the performance of a lifetime but now I felt more like a sick, dizzy failure. I tried to snap out of it by drinking a lot of water and eating some fruit. We were all to meet and run a little practice before the game. I looked hopefully at my team and wished we could've started that night over again. If the coaches knew what we'd done the night before they would've been very disappointed. The work we'd put in to get there was sizable and we'd then done something as stupid as partying the night before our most important game of the year.

o o o

I started to feel a little better before the game. The energy inside the Dome gave us a huge boost as soon as we walked in. I looked at it this way: the game is going to be played whether we were ready or not, so it was best to be as ready as possible. In an attempt to rehydrate, I was drinking so much water that I could hear and feel the water sloshing in my stomach.

Ready or not, it was game time. Months ago, at the start of the season, I'd hoped we would be in this position. I couldn't believe we were there. At the start of the game we were going back and forth for the most part. They scored a touchdown and ended up stopping us on the next drive. The defense had a tough time stopping the quarterback who was quick enough to do trick plays that left our defense on their heels the whole time. In the second quarter I broke up the middle, juked one guy and spun away from another guy and landed in the end zone. I scored a big touchdown but I paid a small price. I'd hit the turf head-first and blacked out for a few seconds. I'd also lost my shoe when I'd spun from the defender. As I came to, I realized I'd scored a touchdown. I ran over to the sideline a little dizzy but okay. I sat on that sideline while the defense was out there on the field. I was exhausted and so disappointed in myself. I had scored a touchdown and become a leader on the field, but I wasn't much of a leader off the field when it came to making the poor choice to drink alcohol the night before a big game. I was going to do everything I could to compensate. I ran hard, regardless of how exhausted I was. We trailed most of the game; the Walton quarterback was giving us a lot of trouble. I could see our defense was very tired, so I figured I'd get up and cheer them on and let them know the sideline had their backs. I ran in for another touchdown in the fourth quarter, but we were still trailing. Time was running out and our chance to win a championship felt as if it was slipping away. We were down 28–12 in the fourth and it seemed we needed a miracle if we were going to win this game. I ran a late touchdown and gained us the two-point conversion. Walton got the ball back and we did everything we could to stop them, but we had nothing left. They ran the clock down and we were not victorious that day. I did everything I could to hold back the tears, but they came anyway. I don't think I was upset that we lost the game; rather, I was upset because we hadn't given ourselves the best chance to win. We'd already lost that game the moment we stepped on that field because of our actions the night before. I still believe

Championship Year High School

- - - - - - - - - - - - - - - - - - - -

1994

the better team did not win. I truly believe that it was only the more prepared team that won. We all learned a lesson that night and it cost us a championship to learn it. I was named co-player of the game, sharing the award with the running back from Walton. I didn't know they ever split an award like that—if they were going to split it with anybody, it should've been with the quarterback—he was simply amazing the way he'd hid the ball. He'd kept our defense on the run and confused all night, from the first play to the last. If it wasn't for his trickery, we would've won that game.

We received our reward, met as a team, and then prepared to head back home. I was very proud of our guys for making it as far as we did. Some of the choices we made had probably cost us the trophy, but we were a championship team and that was decided before the season had even started. And as for my personal dream? I broke the NYS rushing record, rushing with 2,551 yards and 48 touchdowns. Needless to say, I was pleased.

○ ○ ○

Now that football was over, it was time to focus on school and track season. School work was really a struggle during football season and I'd had to learn to balance football, school work, working out, and the correspondence courses I had still been taking. My talent for football gave me the confidence to believe I could make it in the NFL. My struggle with school work placed doubt in my heart that made it difficult for me to believe I'd make it. I knew I wasn't about to let my mother down, so I worked hard and received extra help yet again. The teachers were very good and even stayed late for me to finish. It was necessary for me to do these things if I wanted to graduate. I was hoping to get a scholarship to play D1 football and now had letters from just about every school in the country. I soon had college scouts coming to school to talk to me. It was a blessing for me to be receiving letters from D1 schools regarding football when just ten years prior I couldn't walk.

o o o

I really liked Florida State; they were a championship team with a lot of energy; I loved everything about them and they had wanted me to play football for them. I called the school and I told them I wanted to attend and proceeded to ask if I could talk to Bobby Bowden. The first time I called, they took my name and number. I waited a few days and never heard back from him, so I called again.

"This is Leroy Collins. I want to play for Florida State. Can I talk to Bobby Bowden?" They gave me a different number to call so I hung the phone up and dialed again. A man answered, indicating I was talking to Bobby. I told him who I was and why I was calling, then went into a bit about my school, my position, and my stats. He sounded very impressed.

"We can use a running back like you. How are your grades? Your SAT scores?" I told him my grades were good (and improving every day) but I didn't know anything about the SATs. He suggested I take the exams; they would help me get a scholarship. I was confused about what he was telling me because I never heard anything about an SAT or ACT; my school had never mentioned it to me. I started to get angry because I thought all I had to do was graduate, and then I'd be able to go to any school in the country! I wanted some answers as I wondered why I'd never known this. I had to find out from a coach who was one thousand miles away that I might not have everything I needed to receive a scholarship? I saw my NFL dream dying.

o o o

I asked my guidance counselor about the SATs and told her of my conversation with Bobby Bowden. Then I asked why I'd never been informed of any such test. She told me the exams were optional and said that the information had gone home with all students. That all being said, she advised that there was another round of SATs coming up but suggested I plan to study hard because it wasn't going to be easy. I started to worry about the test, trying to figure out how I'd be able to study along with completing my correspondence class, which involved a lot of homework. I needed to pass the class to graduate, so the majority of my focus went to the classes.

I'd studied a little, as much I could, before sitting for the SAT, but not enough to feel I was truly ready by any means. I walked into the testing room, very nervous, feeling like I was wasting my time (and the school's). After finishing, I asked the proctor when the next exam would be, knowing I probably hadn't done well. That was the last scheduled test of the year, she said, and suggested I could probably take a private course if I didn't do well. I understood about 30 percent of the questions so I'd mostly guessed when it came to the questions I didn't understand. I knew I couldn't waste too much time stressing over it; pass or fail, I still needed to graduate, and I had a lot of work ahead of me.

I turned my focus on graduating and finishing my correspondence courses, and I was feeling good about the direction I was headed. I'd really turned my grades around and learned a lot in a short time despite the fact that I had to work harder than other students to even stay "average."

When I got my SAT results, they weren't good, and I really didn't know what that meant for college. I remembered Coach Bowden telling me I needed to do well on the SATs to receive a scholarship. I talked to several D1 schools and they told me I would have to go to a junior college for two years and then transfer to a D1. I had no other option but to go to a junior college. I was too late in the year to study for another go at the SATs, and the D1 schools were already putting their scholarship offers out. I talked with Boston College and they suggested I go to a school in Franklin, Massachusetts, called Dean Junior College. They said they'd scout me from there so that made me feel better, knowing I still had a chance to play in the NFL further on down the road.

I called Florida State and told them what school I thought I might be going to, so they'd know where to look for me in two years. Florida State suggested I go to a school in Mississippi. I told my mother I wanted to go to the school at Eastern Mississippi because Florida State would pick me up after my first two years. My mother didn't want me to go to Eastern Mississippi. She really tried to convince me not to go, citing the fact that she questioned my safety there without her nearby. I wasn't concerned about the distance because Florida State wanted me, so that's where I wanted to be. My mother thought Dean Junior College would be a better choice because it was only a couple of hours away from home and she would be able to see me.

As the end of the year approached, I had to decide on a school. Against my better judgment, I was going to Dean. I obviously didn't get the D1 scholarship I was hoping for, but I still had an opportunity—my journey was far from over.

o o o

I finished my courses and school was going well. I was waiting for my grades and I thought I'd done well but had an obvious curiosity as to whether I had enough credits to graduate. Being told my grades were "on their way" from my correspondence classes, it was the day before graduation and I still wasn't sure I was going to graduate! Nobody was telling me anything! I was given a cap and gown but I was clueless as to whether I'd even be wearing it.

My counselor told me that although they didn't have my grades, I could still walk the stage with my class. I just wouldn't receive an actual diploma until my grades were finalized. Everything I'd worked for had come down to one grade. The dream I'd had as a little boy, the goal I'd set as an eight-year-old all came down to this. And I was too embarrassed to tell anyone. I was a high school star running back who had broken the NYS rushing record . . . I was the guy that colleges had come to see. I'd received letters from almost every school in the country and yet, I might not graduate. That was an awful feeling.

I sat on the stage waiting for my name to be called that day, ready to walk up and shake the hand of the principal and receive my envelope. I was a nervous wreck, thinking my name wouldn't be called. I sat there praying, wanting to make it out of there without feeling humiliated. I was feeling hopeless as I thought back to the guidance counselor telling me I wouldn't graduate on time and my mother fighting to find me a way. I thought about when I'd been challenged in class and found it in me to speak up for myself and change my situation. I reflected on that period in my life when I couldn't walk, and yet football was always my sport of choice. Instead of accepting weakness, I'd found strength and gone after my dream. I knew my worth. I truly believed I had more to offer than people were realizing. I had no idea what it was, but I felt a sense a power even as a young boy.

I sat on that stage just thinking to myself. Then I heard it. My heart started to beat hard and my hands started to shake as I heard the principal say, "Let's give a round of applause to graduate Leroy Collins, Class of 1995." The crowd went wild—it reminded me of football season. I got emotional as I walked toward the principal. All the struggles, the letdowns, the fights, the beliefs, the disbeliefs, the injuries, the misunderstandings, the challenges, the honor, the dishonor . . . it all came out of me on that walk to the principal. As I fought to hold back tears I cracked a smile and high-fived my classmates on my way back to my seat. I sat in my seat and opened the envelope—it was empty, just as I'd been told it would be. I walked the stage, but I hadn't "officially" graduated yet, with a remaining chance that I still might not graduate after all.

My mother maintained her faith in me, believing in me so much that she started to plan a party. Thankfully we didn't have to wait long because on Tuesday morning, my scores came in and yes, I'd passed. I was now an official high school graduate—a college student. I did what they said I couldn't do. I had climbed mountains I had no business climbing. I fought the fight that they said I couldn't win. With faith, resilience, and lots of support, I graduated high school and was on my way to college. What I didn't know at the time was that what I'd accomplished would affect people. I had a lot of kids looking up to me, wanting to follow in my footsteps. I did my best to provide a good example for all the kids coming up behind me, and I told them to never give up on their dreams and never listen to anybody else when they had a passion or desire to do something.

o o o

I felt worthy of a graduation party now that I was an official graduate. I invited all my family and friends in the neighborhood; it was packed. My youngest sister, one of my five siblings, is a great singer, so my mother asked her to sing me a special song for the occasion. I had no idea what the song would be until my mother gathered everybody together and asked my sister to the mic. My mother had asked my sister to sing Mariah Carey's *Hero* because she said I was hers. I started to tear up before my sister even started singing. My mother had no idea what she'd always meant to me. She was my strength, my supporter, my teacher, and my biggest fan. I know without her love for God and her prayers, I never would have made it as far as I already had. Then, with the most beautiful voice, my sister started singing her heart out. My mother cried and while I was trying to be strong and not cry myself with so many eyes on me, it was clear that half the party was crying, so I let the tears flow—it had been a long road and that was an amazing moment. After all I'd gone through and to think of what I'd accomplished, I felt like a hero.

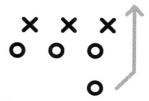

Defeated the Odds

That summer was going to be a special one for me. I reminded myself that I'd done what many had said was impossible—I came back from the dead. I had been blessed during that young time in my life when my vegetative state from that horrific accident had been reversed and I'd ultimately not only learned to walk again after being crippled for over a year, but also I was outrunning guys on the football field left and right. I'd graduated high school when I'd been told that I'd never do it. Then I was told I'd never go on to go to college because I wasn't smart enough and I'd never play college football because I wasn't good enough; I was too small. I was told that while I'd dominated the field in high school, college would be a much different story.

Sometimes I'd only hear rumors of people saying these things and other times they'd tell me directly to my face. I often heard this small voice whisper in my ear telling me, "You can do it; just keep moving forward." I've heard this small voice all my life. Even if I think back all the way to the time when I was in the hospital bed all those years ago, this small voice said, "Get up. You can do it." And I did. I learned to listen to that voice and it pulled me through during a time when I wanted to give up. When there were times I thought I had anything left, that small voice would come to me and say, "Keep going." I've always believed that it's been God speaking to me leading me through my life. That small voice has never let me down.

I was now on my way to college and I wanted to prove to everybody who had ever given up hope on me, or didn't believe in me, wrong. It seemed like I'd spent my young life doing just that and it felt like I was going to continue proving people wrong for the rest of my life.

o o o

I had big plans for the summer of 1995. I knew that was the year I was going to have to work out harder than I had ever worked out before in my life, really pushing myself to the physical limits. The first few weeks of the summer were going exactly as I had planned. I was up bright and early each morning running hills, lifting weights, and catching passes. I felt like I was right on track.

Then I received a letter from Dean Junior College informing me that I had to attend the college orientation program that started four weeks before the regular school year started. It was a special summer acceptance program that I had been accepted into due to my low grades, so I had no choice but to attend. This program was one designed mainly to get students prepared for college before the campus was in full swing and crawling with students. It was part of the agreement the coach had made with the school so it would better my chances of getting accepted. When I'd applied the first time it didn't go through and I was trying everything I could to get in. It was all new and confusing for me. When I was in high school I couldn't wait to get out and then I found myself fighting to get into school and was willing to pay for it. I was on a mission and I knew it would be a long road ahead that would require me to go through college so not getting accepted at first was a little scary. I'm glad the coach went to bat for me but it cut my workout plan short to get in the best shape of my life. I could only hope there was a gym or a place I could work out available when I got there so I could continue my journey.

A few days before I was scheduled to leave I was getting a little nervous. I was going to be on my own—something I'd never done in my life. I'd always had my mother there when I needed her. If ever there was a battle that needed to be fought, Mom had been my army. When I needed prayer, she was my prayer warrior. Now that I was moving away Mom wasn't going to be right there and I had mixed feelings on the whole thing. In fact, I almost backed out of college, not just due to being away from my mother, but due to my sudden fear of the unknown. I was about to jump into unexplored waters as far as I was concerned.

It was a close one the day before I had to go to college. I had just enough time to pack my clothes and put them in a bag. As I went along through the house I grabbed things I was taking with me and threw them in the bag as well. Then I went for a jog and started thinking. *No one says I really have to leave. I can probably just stay home (it'd be easier) and go to Columbia- Greene Community College and play for the Hudson Viking semipro football team and then make it to the NFL, right?*

I ended up going to a friend's house to hang out that day— hide out is probably a more accurate phrase since I knew my parents wanted me home because I had to get up early to get to Massachusetts. I just refused to go home, thinking if I went missing for a couple of days and I didn't show up on time, the school would end up denying my acceptance. I really didn't know what to do. I just didn't want to fail and I couldn't help feeling that if I was there living on my own I would fail. I was hiding out all day and all night. I wasn't planning on going home until I heard that small familiar voice that said, "Go home." I did my best to ignore it and continued to hide out at my friend's house drinking beer until I heard it again. "Go Home." Realizing that I could ignore the voice once but probably not twice, I decided to listen and head home. And in that instant, the moment I gave in to the voice, it was like the fear to go away to college had melted away.

Needless to say, when I finally got home my mother was upset. She had been riding all over town looking for me. I couldn't tell her I'd actually considered quitting before I'd even started and thought about staying home and not going to college. I knew it would have broken her heart so I told her I had been spending time that day saying goodbye to my friends. I only got a few hours of sleep but when I woke up I wasn't just ready to start the day, I was ready to go to college. I grabbed my three Hefty bags of clothes, tossed them in the car, and we were on our way. We all got in the car and headed to Franklin, Massachusetts, which was a little over two-and-a-half hours away.

Reaching the campus, we walked around a bit to check everything out. I had a map of the campus and an itinerary to let us know when things were going to start. There was a meet and greet that gave the parents a clear understanding of what the summer program was all about, and they served finger foods and drinks and they had speakers come up and talk all about Dean Junior College. After the meet and greet we had paperwork to sign before we could bring our things to our rooms to unpack. There weren't that many kids in this particular program; maybe one hundred students. The school gave us the option to have our own room for the four weeks of the program but when actual college started we all would have to move to our dorms with a roommate. I chose to have a room to myself, but in the area that was closest to the athletic fields.

I brought my three garbage bags full of stuff to my room and took one final walk around the campus with my parents before they headed back home. I walked them to the car and gave everyone hugs. As I hugged my mother she started to cry. "I love you, Roy. You're going to do great things because God will always be with you, you know that?"

I could feel the tears welling up in my eyes and I held them back as long as I could before I said, "Thanks, Mom. I know." And with that, a tear fell down my cheek and I still remember my lips quivering as I said, "I love you too, Mom."

As the family car started to drive off I knew I couldn't hold it back anymore. I broke down and cried my eyes out as the reality of being on my own set in. I gave a quick wave, not wanting to draw it all out, and headed back to my dorm room so no one would see me cry. Arriving back in my room I sat on the bed and thought, "Now what?" Unable to think of any better plan, I got on my knees and asked God to strengthen and protect me from whatever lie ahead.

The school had a dinner set up for all of us so all the new students could come together to meet and get to know each other. I was skeptical about going to the dinner. I wasn't sure if I was ready to open myself up to meeting new people. I was used to the people I'd grown up around because they knew me, they know my story, and I was comfortable around them. I was entering a whole new world that I wasn't comfortable with, and I was alone. Ultimately I decided to go to the dinner and I met a couple of guys who were on the football team. I knew they were football players because they had their high school football jerseys on. I introduced myself and they looked at me in disbelief, as if they didn't believe who I was, and I really didn't understand why at first.

"Do you mean to tell us you're the same Leroy Collins who broke the New York State rushing record?"

"Yeah, that's me."

"Wow, you were so good in high school that I thought you were going on to a Division 1 school," one guy said.

"Well, if I had my way, I would be, but I'm here for now," I said. "Truth is, I didn't do so well on my SATs so I didn't get an offer to go D-1. I'm taking the JC route to start and my goal is to work hard so I do get that D-1 offer. Gotta do what you gotta do, right?"

"Everyone I know has followed you, watching your stats all year," another guy piped up. "We used to talk about you all the time."

"Yeah," agreed another guy, "but somehow I thought you'd be bigger . . ."

We all laughed. I couldn't believe I was sitting here hundreds of miles from home in a different state, and I was running into guys who not only knew who I was, but people who had been talking about me!? It was then that I realized I never really gave myself much credit in thinking anyone outside of little Hudson, New York, would know much about me.

I guess I made a good impression on those guys that day, or intimidated them, because one of the guys laughed and said, "Well, I guess I know I'm not playing this year!"

"What? Why do you say that?" I said.

"Because I'm a running back and I'm pretty sure I probably can't start over you!"

I didn't really know what to say in response because of course I planned on starting. Little did anyone know I was on a mission and I had just two years to make a good impression.

As the dinner went on we all got to know each other a little better and I asked them where they were from. One was a linebacker and the other was a running back, both from Connecticut. I was glad I went to the dinner and I'd met those guys. It made the transition to being away from home a little easier when I was sharing my main interest with guys who could relate. We talked football the entire dinner and planned to start working out together to get ready for the season. I decided that night that this turned out to be a pretty good start to college and a good start to meeting new people.

As I went back to my room that night I was eager to call my mother and fill her in on the guys who knew who I was and let her know about the classes I was going to be taking. I believed I was prepared for college, given all the classes I'd taken over the last couple of years—they'd been intense and came with a lot of pressure so I was sure I could handle whatever was coming my way now. It really felt like everything I'd gone through in high school and all of the hard work I'd put in had been preparing me for this very moment. Mom was glad to hear that things were going so well and she assured me that if I needed anything, she was there as always, but she had every confidence that I was going to be alright.

o o o

The summer program was four weeks long and football practice started right after it so I was going to make sure I took full advantage of every day to prepare myself for the upcoming season.

The first day of classes was a little different from anything I'd known in high school. In my first class, the teacher gave all the students the entire lesson plan for the four weeks. I was blown away knowing what I was going to be doing for the next month, so I planned on getting a jump start on all my lessons where I could, figuring I'd play things from the front instead of always feeling like I'd been running behind back in high school.

I had three classes a day during that summer, all of them running an hour-and-a-half long. Once I had the first day under my belt I was ready to work out so I headed to the gym. When I got there I discovered it was locked and I tried to find someone to open it but was told the gym was closed for the summer. Keeping my training plan in mind, I wasn't about to accept that. I already felt like I was behind on my training since my summer break had been cut short with this summer school. It took me a few days to get a hold of the coach but when I did I explained that I'd found a few other players who wanted to work out with me as well and he was able to pull some strings to have the gym open for us during certain hours of the day. We couldn't go every day, but I ran and found plenty of other things to do on the days I couldn't work out in the gym.

o o o

Summer school was going well and I stuck to my plan to study and do my best to stay ahead of the scheduled lessons. It wasn't easy but I was finding ways to be more regimented and keep on top of everything. Before I knew it the summer school program was coming to an end. Summer break wasn't over yet but I noticed students coming in who hadn't been there for the previous four weeks. I figured some of the guys that came in were football players and the girls that were arriving were most likely soccer players.

It was a few days before our football orientation and I didn't feel like I was ready to play just yet. I'd been working out but not as much as I'd originally wanted due to the weight room schedule. We had our first football orientation and received our schedule for the year. I was so excited that I was on a college football team. I got the chance to meet all the players that first day and it seemed there were some returning players there mixed in with some first-year players as well. Everybody was nice but it seemed that the freshmen were going to be sticking together for now. I had to remind myself that yes, I was on the team, but I wasn't "official" until summer school ended and I'd passed everything. Until then I was permitted to sit in on meetings but I couldn't practice. While it bummed me out to not play with the guys right away, I looked at it as positively as possible, realizing I had a chance to see my competition in action before they got a chance to see me play. A lot of the players seemed to have heard about me or seen films of me but had never seen me in person.

o o o

I was thankful to find out that at the end of summer school I'd passed everything and received the credits I needed to keep my acceptance letter. I was now official and could practice with the team. Marking the end of summer school meant it was time for all the summer school students who were athletes like me to move to our regular dorms. Those who weren't pursuing a sport were asked to go home for a week prior to the fall semester starting. I had to move into a dorm that was all the way on the other side of campus, pretty far away from everything. The dorm I'd been in during summer school had been perfect; it was close to the café, not too far from the gym, and near the student rec center as well. When I found out where I'd now be I requested a room change before the other students showed up but my request was denied. They couldn't make any changes until all the students who were registered reported for classes.

It was the weekend before the start of school and everyone was arriving to move in to the dorms and unpack their bags. It was incredible for me to watch students bring boxes and boxes of belongings including stereos, TVs, and multiple suitcases into their dorm rooms. I was fascinated because all I'd brought was my three Hefty bags full of clothes and personal items. I realized I'd never been in a position before where it was emphasized that I had so little. I had what everybody in my community had, so I'd never known any differently, or realized what I may have been missing. During those first four weeks I was there if I wanted to watch TV I had to go to the student rec center; if I wanted to play video games I went to somebody else's room to play. All I'd had in my room for the four-week summer program were books, an alarm clock, and pictures of my family, in addition to a folder that was important to me—one full of football articles from high school along with a few letters from the D-1 schools to remind of where I was going. I believe I'd done as well as I had in summer school because I didn't have much in my room to distract me, allowing me to focus.

By the time the caravan of students came in to unpack their bags and dress up their rooms, I was getting ready for my first college practice. I was a little nervous after having watched them practice, seeing how fast they were and how hard they hit. I could only hope I was ready to play at that level. I'd had a lot of critics growing up and I just didn't want the criticism to affect me when I stepped out onto that field.

My first day ended up not being so bad at all. I felt fast and strong, and although I didn't have football pads yet, just a helmet, I believed I was going to fit right in. The other players on the team seemed amazed by how fast I was and it wasn't long before they wanted me to race the fastest guy on the team, someone who had held the record for the fastest player on the team just the year before. We agreed to race at a time when we were both fresh so it would be a fair race.

I went back to my dorm room from practice feeling more confident and optimistic, like things were looking good for me. Arriving to my room that day I was greeted by my new room-mate. He was with his parents unpacking all his stuff (and boy, did he have a lot of stuff). We all introduced ourselves despite the fact they were surprised to see me. They'd been under the impression they would be the first ones in the room because the school hadn't notified him that he'd have a roommate. I filled them in on the fact that I was on the football team and we'd started practice a week prior, as well as the fact that I'd had to attend a summer program before I started.

The way our dorm room was set up, I had more windows on the side I'd chosen. Naturally he asked if he could have my side of the room because he wanted his desk and bed near a window. I explained that he could easily have it in a few days because I was due to move to the other side of campus. It really seemed that they were bothered by the fact that I'd gotten there before they did, and I'd chosen a particular side; this was all new to me. And based on the things this guy brought with him, it seemed pretty obvious that he didn't ever want or plan on a roommate. This guy wasn't into sports at all so I didn't believe it would've been a good match even if I had been staying in that dorm. Surprising to me, it actually turned out to be pretty good.

After a few days went by I asked to have my room changed but was told they were still expecting more students to move in, so they denied me once again. They told me they'd send out a room change form to students like me who wanted their room changed, but that I should be aware it was on a first-come, first-served basis. I was told I "wasn't on the top of the list," and that was probably because I hadn't known there was one. So, in the meantime, I just dealt with walking clear across the campus to class and all the activities that were taking place.

Football practice was going great and I was competing with one of the second-year players for the starting position. He was pretty good and much bigger than I was but I believed I was faster and I think I was a better running back. The coach said it was an open competition and no starters had been determined as of yet. I thought that was a good way to get the guys working harder and it gave us a chance to bring out the best in us.

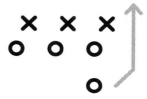

Injured Spirit

I finally got my pads and I was ready to show everybody what I could do. It was the start of a practice and the guy I'd planned to race came to me said he was ready if I was. "I'm always ready," I said, hoping I exuded the confidence to not only intimidate him, but also to pump myself up. Everyone gathered round—the whole team and the coaches, as some of our teammates had been hyping it up. It was to be a fifty-yard race and the start was decided to be, "Ready, down, set, go." One of the players threw a hand up and said, "Ready, down, set, hut!" and we both just threw that false start off until another player said it: "Ready, down, set, go!" (Not hut.) We both took off and he had a very fast start. He started the race off in the lead because he was so quick to get out of the gate but I started to pick up speed and gained on him. We got where we only had about twenty more yards to go until I kicked it up a notch and got within one step of his lead. When we reached the ten-yard mark I skated by him.

The team went crazy! If they hadn't known me before, then they knew me now, because I'd just beaten the guy they said was the fastest, best athlete on the team. And I didn't just beat him; I'd caught him from behind. Despite the fact that I'd stumbled on my start, I still managed to beat him to the finish. I didn't want to take his crown to make him feel less then what he was. I was in a direct competition and I wanted the coaches to notice me so I refused to lose. I had to win that race knowing they had asked me to race their best guy because they obviously saw something in me that they liked. If I would've lost, my chance of garnering more respect would've been slimmer. Nobody knew I was on a mission to the NFL but as I listened to all the guys around me it was obvious that I wasn't the only one on my team with big ambitions. I was wondering how many other football players had my same NFL dream. I did a little casual research and came to discover that my entire team had some hope or dream of making it to the pros. Maybe I'm not so unique with this dream, I thought. I soon came to realize that it was a pretty common high school or college athlete's dream to one day play a professional sport. I thought about all the schools in the world and all the football players having the same dream I did and it felt like it diminished the importance of my goal a bit. Where I was from, I was the only one with this dream. But I wasn't in Hudson anymore.

I had to remind myself that I'd had this dream to play professional football since I was eight years old; and not just any eight-year-old boy, but a broken one at the time. I'd been holding on to this dream for most of my life through some pretty rough times, and it was sometimes the idea of having this hope that had helped me through it all. I started to doubt myself—not my ability in general, I knew I was good—but my chances of actually making it to the NFL with so many others having the same dream. How can almost every high school football player in the country want what I wanted and have the same dream? Certainly, we couldn't all expect to make it; that would be impossible. One person had to dream harder than the next and work harder than the others if they wanted to make it to the pros. I secretly told myself that I would be that guy and I asked God for the strength I needed to push forward.

o o o

I resolved to work on running as fast and as hard as I could in practice, and each day after team practice I would go to the weight room and then run sprints late into the night. I committed to doing this every day, trying to work harder than everybody else. I wanted to work harder than the people I knew and was seeing train every day. Heck, I wanted to work harder than the people I didn't even know and never saw. Practice was easy for me because I had my blinders on with my sights focused only on the NFL.

I ended up winning the starting position at running back. "This is my chance to reinforce the confidence in my dream," I thought. As we got within just a few days of our first game, I ran hills and ran all around campus with strength shoes on. They were supposed to give me more bounce when I ran, making me run faster. I had those strength shoes on all the time in an effort to make my workout more challenging.

It was game day when Coach told me the second-year running back would be splitting time with me—I really didn't want to hear that. I had big plans for this game and none of them included splitting time. I felt good; I was confident and strong and I was ready to make a good impression and leave my mark.

Leroy Sr and Leroy Jr at Dean Jr College

1995

The game started off very well. We were winning and I'd had a few big runs. I hadn't scored a touchdown yet but I was gaining big yards. It was in the second quarter that I got the ball, broke up the middle, and cut to the right. I shook off one defender and I could see the end zone . . . I was going to score my first touchdown in college football! Then suddenly I heard a pop! and I went down fast, untouched. Everything went silent as I tried to get up and fell back down. Within moments a horrible pain shot down my leg. Looking down to assess the damage, my knee was so big and instantly swollen, I grabbed it and started streaming. I didn't know what had happened—nobody had touched me, yet I went down. I was just running for a touchdown with no one around me and my knee popped. The coaches and the team trainer ran over to check me out, noting my knee was clearly in bad shape. They picked me up and carried me to the sideline to have a further look. When I got up the whole stadium cheered for me, reminding me of when I'd been carried off the field in a stretcher in high school. They all cheered and clapped and I gave them a thumbs-up. I could only hope everything was fine.

As I sat on the sideline getting examined there were so many things running through my head. *What if my leg is broken and I can never play again?* I tried to remain positive, believing everything was fine and I'd be back out there the following week. I was thinking I'd ice it and rest up during halftime, to come back in the third quarter. I was just really hoping my season wasn't over. As I sat on the sideline the trainer made me do a few tests to see if she could figure out what the problem might be. Much to my dismay, my knee was getting bigger before my eyes. I asked the trainer if I'd be able to get back out there right away.

"I don't think so," she said. "It looks like you're going to have to see a doctor before we know exactly what's going on."

I was so mad—at whom? I didn't know. I just couldn't believe my first game had ended early after all I'd been through and all the training I'd done. They wouldn't know exactly what was wrong with my knee until I got X-rays so they just wrapped my knee with ice to bring the swelling down and gave me crutches in the meantime.

So, for now, I really didn't know if my season was over or if I was going to be back in a few weeks. I didn't know what to do. I sat in my room praying that everything was going to be fine and hoping I'd get the chance to play. As luck would have it, I finally got my request for a room change—talk about bad timing. I got a room on the other side of campus in the same area I'd been in during the summer school. Thankfully I didn't have much to carry aside from my bags of clothes. It was just a few bags but it was on the other side of campus and I knew it would be a long walk with crutches. I was happy at the idea of being much closer to everything and near the area where most of the football players lived but I needed to figure out how to get there. I was going to ask one of the players to help me with my bags but I was too embarrassed to ask anyone. All I had was three garbage bags of clothes and I didn't want anyone's pity or to be made fun of. I decided to wait for my roommate and told him the room was all his and he was now free to have my side of the room.

I'd only had one incident with my roommate during the time we were together. My alarm clock had gone off and I didn't wake up so he reached over me to turn it off without waking me up. I let him have it after I woke up late for class. I told him not to ever do that again and that was the end of it. I was now happy to be moving but still had to figure out how I was going to get my bag on the other side of campus without someone seeing me and without asking for help. I didn't have to move until the next morning so I laid down to rest because my knee was hurting so bad. I called my mother and told her what had happened. She was hoping just as I was that everything would be fine. There wasn't much she could do but pray for me.

"Roy, you know I wish I could be there," she said.

"I know, Mom. I'll be fine," I assured her. "Just keep me in your prayers."

The next morning my roommate helped me carry my bags to my new dorm room. My new roommate wasn't there so I went in and just started unpacking and putting clothes away. I had no idea who I'd be living with but whoever he was, he played on the football team.

o o o

I was hoping to hear some news that next day about an appointment for my knee. I went to see the team trainer to ask some questions because it was really hard sitting still not knowing. I needed to know something. She told me to be patient and she would let me know when the doctor could get me in for X-rays. A week passed before I heard anything. I finally got in for them to take some images and I didn't receive the news I was hoping to hear.

"Well, it looks like you're going to need surgery, young man." I think I just stared at him in disbelief.

"What is it?" I said, trying to hide my instant panic.

"The tendon in your patella is torn, I'm afraid."

"So, what does that mean? When will I be able to go back to football?"

"You might be done for the year," he said.

I was crushed and before I knew what was going on I cried in that doctor's office as I saw all my dreams and hard work going down the drain. I was so devastated. This was something that was completely beyond my control and there was nothing I could do about it. I'd worked so hard and had big plans for this season. This was a huge blow I definitely didn't expect. Instead of me suiting up to get ready for a football game I'd be walking onto the field on crutches. I felt so low; everybody around me felt my pain. "You've always got next year," they said. "It's okay, man. Just shake it off." It was nearly impossible for me to think ahead to next year when I'd had so much hope for this season. It was hard to focus on anything else.

I watched those next games from the sideline thinking of all the things I would have done if I'd been out there on the field. It got to the point where it was hard for me to watch any more of the game so I hobbled into the locker room to sit on the bench, replaying the incident in my head. I started thinking that maybe I'd pushed myself too hard. I was on a mission I'd refused to give up on even on the days when I found myself exhausted as I ran hills. When it was late at night and everybody was tucked away asleep I was out running sprints. I don't know, maybe I pushed my body to a breaking point. What other explanation could there be for me to go down like I had when nobody had been around to touch me? I sat there in that locker room until the guys came in for halftime and then I stepped out until they were ready to go back out on the field.

Thinking back to when I'd first gotten to school I'd felt alone but I had football and that made me feel like I had a place in this school. Now that I didn't have football I felt a bit out of place. I went home to visit and stayed a few days longer than I should've. I just felt more comfortable at home around my family and felt that was what I needed at that time. Even when I got back to campus I realized I was skipping class more and traveling home a lot more. There were even times I went home to Hudson and didn't even let my mother know. Clearly she would not have approved of me leaving school as much as I did. My grades were slipping and I was also slipping further and further into depression. Not having the opportunity to play football was not working out for me.

o o o

I'd become friends with some guys that weren't on the football team and it seemed like all they did was drink, play video games, and smoke weed. I was mostly hanging out with them to play video games because I didn't have a TV, let alone a video game system. I drank with them sometimes but I never smoked weed. I saw what that was doing to some close friends and family and I didn't want that happening to me. But I did drink more than a kid with an NFL dream should have.

It wasn't long before I found myself hanging out with these guys and girls all the time, and I was now walking better with less pain so I'd ditched the crutches because I was traveling all over the place. I had still been going to practice every day until I started hanging with my new crew. Then I totally stopped going to practice and football started to slip away off my radar as I admittedly seemed to forget what I was going to school for—it wasn't about going to classes or going to practice any longer.

I had the date for my surgery and I missed that appointment because I went home to Hudson. The team trainer called my mother and told her I had a date for my surgery set and I had never showed. My mother called my dorm and left me a message. I was afraid to call her back because I knew I'd messed up. So, I avoided calling her but I knew Thanksgiving break was coming and I was going to see her in just a week anyway. I had a conference with my teachers and they let me know what I would have to do if I planned on returning for the next semester. I had to do well on my exams and term paper, no question about it. I was so far behind I wasn't sure if I even had it in me to try to catch up by putting in the extra study time to pass these tests or finish my term paper. As I had had to do back when I was in high school, I knew I had to find it in myself to ask for help, knowing I couldn't do it on my own. Thankfully, I got the help I needed because I had less than a month to finish a ten-page term paper and to complete and pass two exams. I made the decision it was time to buckle down and study for the exams and the paper. The last thing I wanted was to get expelled so I put my mind toward gaining some of my focus back.

○ ○ ○

One of my old buddies from my hometown came to my school to hang out with me right before Thanksgiving break. He was with me for about three days before I had to leave but I'd already bought a bus ticket. He took a bus up to the college but he didn't have a ticket to get back to Hudson so we had to see if he could get a ticket on the same bus I was set to take. The bus I was taking was already full but there was one scheduled to go to Albany a few hours later that had seats available. I was able to switch my bus in order to ride the one to Albany with him. While we waited for that bus my buddy knew I didn't smoke so he told me he was going to take a walk quick and hit a blunt (smoke weed). "I'll come with you," I offered.

"Nah, you don't smoke weed . . . You're a big football star."

"I'm not a football star tonight. I wanna hit the blunt," I said. We walked outside and headed down the street so he could light up. He took a few hits and passed it to me. This was my first experience smoking weed so I didn't know the ins and outs to smoking. I inhaled and blew it out right away.

"Nah, man . . . you gotta take a good inhale and hold it for a few seconds before you blow it out."

I took another crack at it, this time drawing it deep into my lungs and holding it for a few seconds before accidentally swallowing and feeling like I was going to cough up a lung. I was coughing so bad that I couldn't take another hit, and just when I'd think the coughing fit was over it would start up again. We walked back to the bus station and I was so dizzy that I had to sit down. My buddy thought it was funny and went on to razz me about how I'd gotten buzzed off just one hit. It wasn't long before I was thirsty, hungry, and sleepy—in that order. We got something to eat from a store in the bus station. I had a grape drink, a bag of onion rings, and some Debbie's cupcakes—snacks never tasted so good. We ate while we waited for the bus and I was getting tired so I had to keep telling myself not to fall asleep, but I lost that battle. As luck would *not* have it, we both fell asleep in the bus station and we ended up totally missing the bus. I woke my buddy up five hours later to discover our bus had left three hours earlier.

I was running around the bus station, totally tripping out. They'd already changed my ticket once and I was thinking that they might not do it for me again. "You don't understand," I explained to the casher, "I have to make it home. My family is expecting me."

I was told not to worry because there would be another bus in a few hours and we could get on that one. I waited for the bus, free of any "chemical recreation" whereas I was not going to miss the bus again. I was totally focused now. The bus came a few hours later and I made it home.

When I got home the first thing I did was look for some suitcases, or even some bigger duffel bags to take back with me. I was now coming home almost every weekend after my injury. Nobody really missed me aside from my mother and grandmother because as far as my friends were concerned I was always around. When I came home on weekends (or sometimes even during the week) I would just stay at friend's houses and instruct them to keep my visit a secret.

My mother drilled me about my missed operation. "Roy, why didn't you tell me you had a date for your knee surgery? Why did I have to find out about it only after they called me to say you didn't show up? Why would you miss that?"

"I dunno, Mom. I guess I was nervous. You know all those months I spent in the hospital as a kid. All I can think of is having those bandages changed every day, the skin ripped off me two or three times a day. Not necessarily good memories," I said.

She understood me but what she didn't understand is why I had kept her out of the loop. "But why wouldn't you tell me so I could be there with you?" As I mentally scrambled to come up with a logical explanation, I thought back to how I'd been hoarding the mail regarding insurance information and the operation date because truthfully, I wasn't ready to go under the knife. I felt bad for skipping the surgery and the several appointments that had been made once I found out that my mother was having trouble rescheduling me. If I'd known it was going to give her grief I would've followed through with the appointments and been more considerate.

I've always loved spending time with my family during the holidays, my favorite time of the year. Being with them has always brought joy to my life, and I'm telling you, I needed it. I felt so lost during this time. I was wondering where the young boy who had had so much passion and drive had gone. I had a little boy deep inside me who had once claimed that nothing could stop him—not death, not two broken legs, and not the embarrassment of having scars all over his body. Where did that boy go? The only thing I was now feeling was emptiness, heartache, and pain. I felt like I'd put all I had on the table only to have it all taken from me. I never really had the encouraging words like, "It's going to be okay" or, "You can do it." Even the words "If you try and fail, you just get back up and try again." As much love as I had around me my entire life, I was never showered with those words. They had always come from inside me. With my condition as a little boy whenever I wanted to try something new I would hear things like, "Don't do that, you can get hurt" or, "You're not strong enough to do that" or, "You're not smart enough to do that." (The exceptions being my mother and uncle, of course.) Those were the negative words I'd always tried my best to block out when I was young but now sometimes I found they were creeping their way in. Even when I was one of the best running backs in New York state I would still hear criticism. "He's too small," "He's not fast enough to hang with the college boys." I really didn't know who to turn to when I started feeling like giving up. I didn't think I had anyone to turn to so I didn't bother trying. I just kept my hurt to myself. And as I did so I had no idea I was heading for self-destruction.

o o o

I enjoyed my time with my family at Thanksgiving but it was time for me to go back to school. I wasn't looking forward to it either because I had to finish a term paper and study for tests before the end of the semester. I worked hard on my assignments because I wanted to come back for the second semester. I got all the help I could to make sure I had all my bases covered. I was still hanging out with the crew that lived close to my dorm and we were playing video games one night when one of the girls started smoking weed and passed it around the room. It was headed in my direction and while I thought I never had any intention of ever smoking weed again, instead of letting it pass by like I always had, I hit it. Everybody sat in quiet disbelief because they knew I didn't (and wouldn't) smoke weed, but yet this night had been different. I ended up smoking all night with them (and I didn't cough once) and I was so high I couldn't move. Nights like this soon became a habit and I then found myself smoking weed almost every day. Every time I smoked I would always tell myself, "I shouldn't be doing this." I knew it was wrong and I did it anyway. I never thought I would be in the position of deciding if I should smoke weed or not. It wasn't that long ago that I was waking up at 2:00 a.m. and running sprints. Now I was in a downward spiral. On the plus side, I was getting my school work done as I did spend significant time on my studies and writing papers. It was apparent that I still had at least a little bit of determination left in me. I just wished I could find more will.

Dropping the Hammer

The semester was coming to an end. I'd finished my term paper and I was preparing for my exams since I knew I had to do well if I wanted to come back. I also got an appointment for my knee surgery to take place over Christmas break in Rhode Island, so at least I felt like some things were coming together for me. I took my finals, rushed back to my room to smoke a blunt (alone), and got on the bus to go home for break. I was hoping I'd done well enough to come back next semester, but only time would tell.

My friends back home didn't know I was smoking weed but when I got home the first thing I did was look for friends to smoke with. I went from Mr. Touchdown to being a weed-head, and I hid my secret from everybody except for those I was smoking with. I made sure my mother didn't find out, or any of my close relatives; they would've been so disappointed in me. So, I kept my newfound habit a secret from anyone I knew who wouldn't approve.

I was only able to hang out with my friends from home for about a week before I had to travel to Rhode Island for my surgery. It was going to be an overnight trip and my father drove me to Rhode Island and the school actually paid for the travel and the hotel we were staying in. I was still very nervous about the surgery, and on top of that, I was nervous that the doctor was going to find out I'd been smoking weed and tell my parents. There wasn't much I could do except skip out on the surgery again, and that wasn't going to happen. As I walked into the changing area to prepare for surgery the nurse came in and gave me instructions on how to put my gown on. I thanked her but I couldn't help but remind myself how I had more than enough experience with hospital gowns.

They wheeled me into surgery and hooked me up to all the various machines and began the anesthesia. As I was told to count down from ten I remember saying "10, 9, 8, 7, 6 . . ." and I woke up about two hours later with my knee wrapped up. "Are they still going to do the surgery on my knee?" I asked a nurse.

"You're all set. It's all done and everything went well," she said.

I couldn't believe it. I didn't feel a thing. I didn't know what they were doing to me when I was out, but yet everything turned out great. This was so very different from any other hospital experience I'd ever had. The doctor came in later to explain what he'd done and he assured me I'd be fine and ready to play football the following season. To hear those words surprised me a bit because I had kind of forgotten about football. I couldn't believe I had no reaction, no emotion . . . it was almost like I'd given up on it and hadn't even realized it. It wasn't until then that I became aware of just how far into depression I'd slipped. Football was the thing that had pulled me through a lot of tough times.

○ ○ ○

I needed to snap out of this funk I was in because every time I thought about football I was getting angry and I tried to block it out of my head. The doctor let me go home that same day of my surgery. Knowing we had a long ride home, he gave us instructions as to how I should ride, so I sat in the back seat with my leg up over the front seat and slept the whole way back to Hudson.

Back at home I really didn't feel pain until the next morning. It was then that I was in so much pain that I refused to leave my bed. My mother made sure I had everything I needed and I was laid up in bed for two days—enough time for the rest of my body to start to hurt. I decided to get up and move around and when I did my leg started to bleed, which caused me to panic and call the doctor. I thought I'd ripped my stitches and possibly done more damage to my knee. I was told to clean it and check the stitches; if they were still attached, it would be fine and I shouldn't worry. He told me to just make sure I used my crutches and keep it wrapped. I followed the doctor's instructions and did everything I was supposed to do. But I was still in some pain; so much so that it slowed me down from hanging out with my friends.

Christmas break was ending and it was time to go back to school. I wasn't sure if I'd received the grades I needed to return since I never got anything telling me otherwise but I did receive my course schedule, so I had to assume I'd done alright. Before I went to school I went to one of my friends who knew how to get me some weed and I bought a few ounces to take back to school with me. I had my cousins drive me back that time since I really didn't want to ride the bus with crutches and a bag—it would have been hard to travel. When I got back to school, my cousins stayed for few days. I hadn't ever smoked in front of them because I knew they wouldn't have approved so I avoided hanging with my crew, knowing they would want to smoke. I really couldn't do much, so all we did was hang out in the student lounge or in my room.

When my cousins left I made plans to get together with my crew. I didn't show them all that I had but I brought a few bags so we could smoke it up and make up for lost time. This semester had started off by picking up right where the last semester had ended. I found myself smoking a lot; I also found myself skipping class a lot. I knew I needed help but I didn't know who to reach out to or who could relate to what I was going through. When I was high I would think about it, and when I was sober I would think about it. It was obviously becoming a problem.

One girl I hung out with commented one day on the fact that I always seemed to have weed, and she wanted to know if I had more. I said, "I have a little . . ."

"Well, can I buy some off you by any chance?"

I'd never really thought about selling it before, but I agreed and showed her what I had. "Wow," she said, "I'll go get my money."

"Alright, but please don't tell anybody because I don't really want people knowing I have it," I said. She agreed and came back about ten minutes later with money to buy the weed. "Remember, don't say where you got this from," I reminded her.

Later that night some of the guys from my crew showed up at my room. "Hey, heard you got weed."

"Just a little," I said. "Who told you—Nicole?"

They weren't looking to buy from me since they didn't have money but wanted to smoke, so we did in my room. My roommate was there and I wasn't sure if he smoked. I knew he didn't during football season, but it was the dead of winter and he joined in. I reminded everyone that they couldn't tell anybody because if I got caught I could be expelled—or worse, arrested. I never really thought about how serious it was until I said it out loud. It wasn't just college kids having fun drinking and smoking weed—I could go to *jail*. Now that was all I could think about now—having this illegal drug in my possession and getting caught and serving time. I was almost giving it away just so I get rid of it, I was so terrified. Whenever my roommate wanted some I gave it to him. Whenever my crew wanted some, I gave it to them. Talk about a wake-up call.

○ ○ ○

Weeks went by and my leg was feeling better and I could get around better than I had been. I had no more weed in my possession and I wanted to keep it that way. When someone came to ask me for weed I was now proud to tell them I didn't have any. I still met up with my crew and smoked on occasion but I started to get back in the gym as I was trying to rehabilitate my knee into regaining some strength.

There was a football team meeting about the upcoming season and I wasn't sure if that included me because I hadn't been involving myself in anything the team had going on lately. Then it hit me that I'd completely fallen off the deep end. There was a football meeting and I was seriously considering not going. What was wrong with me?? I started to remember the dreams I'd had as a little boy when I couldn't walk, remembering the goals I'd set for myself when I was still in a wheelchair. "Who have I become?" I thought. I just broke down and cried. I felt like I was battling and fighting something on the inside. Some things were pulling me in one direction while other things were pulling me in another. I don't know what it was but it was a constant fight for survival against my will.

I did go to the team meeting and found out that the coach still had plans for me but he had been notified that I'd been struggling to keep my grades up. I really hadn't applied myself to my studies and yet I knew I had to have a review at the end of the year which would determine whether I will be back. I was so far behind I really felt like I just needed a fresh start and prayed I could get one but with the little time I had left I knew that was impossible. I made up my mind to buckle down and I did the best I could with the time I had left. I wasn't smoking weed as much and I was hanging out with my crew less. Don't get me wrong. I still had my share of fun but I worked harder to stay on a path toward finishing strong.

Looking back at those past few months I was so ashamed of myself to think that I'd let things get as far away from me as they did. I dug deep and fought hard to keep my word to myself. I was more focused and started seeing my purpose again. Looking at how much of a failure I had been, as personally humiliating to me as it was, made me work harder to overcome the challenges I'd created for myself. I finally had a clear head to reflect on all the things I'd been going through. I thought back on all the close calls I'd had; one when the drug dog came to school to sniff things out and was near my room but (thankfully) had no reaction. I would've lost everything and let everybody that counted on me down. I was happy to be back on my feet but I still had school stuff to deal with since I was determined to get good news at my academic conference.

o o o

I did the best I could on my school work for the time I had left. I hadn't done well overall so I was confident they weren't going to let me back in school, although I tried to hope for the best. On the day of my school conference I decided that if I was permitted to continue I would do everything I could to stay. I was hanging with a few friends on conference day and one of them started smoking weed. (Once again, I'd told myself that I didn't plan to ever smoke it again.) But . . . knowing my conference wasn't for another four hours, I took a few drags. I actually got higher than I was hoping to get, and I knew I was in for some trouble. I did everything I could to bring myself down but nothing worked. "You are so, so stupid," was all I kept saying to myself. Whatever they handed down to me at that meeting, I knew I deserved it. At that point I was planning on just skipping it but I went anyway just to face my fate at Dean Junior College.

When I walked into the room I was met by an oval table with all my teachers, the dean of the school, and other staff members in attendance. They asked me to take a seat, so I sat down and they handed me a folder with my name on it as they explained what the meeting was all about, emphasizing that at the end of the meeting they would determine if I was fit to come back next year. As they talked about my participation, they discussed my ups and downs. They addressed my attendance issues and the lack of consistency I'd demonstrated when it came to my homework assignments being handed in. I knew that everything they were saying was all true and I felt so ashamed to hear it laid out like this all at once that I wished I could take it all back. They looked at me as I sat there in silence, unsure what to say and feeling paranoid from the weed, as if they had some idea I was high. I'd used Visine and put a lot of cologne on to mask the smell but I felt they knew something was up.

"Mr. Collins, do you have anything you would like to add?" they asked.

I took a deep breath as I considered my words carefully. "I think I now know where I went wrong and I do feel like I'm working hard now to make some changes in my life. If I can have a second chance to make up for the time I've missed I know I could make the most of it," I implored, hoping I didn't sound like I was begging.

They said they needed to take a vote so I'd had to leave and return in an hour for the verdict. When I got back to the meeting they broke the news to me—I was being expelled. I begged them to give me another chance and still they refused. I left that meeting devastated and angry—not at the school, but angry with myself for having allowed any of this to happen.

o o o

I didn't know what I was going to do now. This wasn't the plan I'd had when I left high school. I was going to go to Dean for two years. It was to be my stepping stone to bigger things. I was going to do well in school and in football and sign a scholarship to play for Florida State. That was my plan. Instead, I hurt my knee and couldn't play football, I'd taken up the habit of smoking weed, and now I'd been kicked out of school.

After I'd gotten hurt I felt so lost and I realized I never really factored in a contingency plan for myself if playing football was ever not in the picture. It was so easy to pick up new habits in college. Most of my life I had always felt that when I was in trouble or making bad decisions I'd had an angel to guide me, to speak to me. But now it had been so long since I'd heard that voice inside me. I didn't hear anything anymore; I didn't feel anything. I felt alone and had to fend for myself. I'd made those poor choices and now I had to live with them, but I didn't know what I was going to tell my mother.

I started by making the absolute decision to stop smoking weed because it was ruining my life and I had so much to live for. With school now over, everyone was packing up and heading home so I went around to say my goodbyes and left for Hudson.

When I got home I broke the heart-wrenching news to my mother, explaining to her that I couldn't return the following year. She obviously wanted to know why, and I told her all about how I'd struggled with the school work and failed too many classes. "But Mom, I've got to find another school—one that has football. It's what keeps me going."

It wasn't long before we found Alfred State College in Alfred, New York, a school that was just going into their second year with a football program. I went for a visit and I liked what I saw. I could envision myself there and was hoping I could attend. I submitted my application and sent it off with a prayer. I was working my bum leg out hard since my surgery and while it was fully healed now, it was so skinny that I had to keep exercising it simply to get its size back.

A few weeks had passed since my Alfred application and I hadn't heard anything yet. I felt like I needed a miracle. I tried to stay busy, working out hard and keeping the faith that everything was going to work out.

○ ○ ○

I finally got the call that Alfred State was accepting me and I was so grateful to be gifted (yes, I felt truly gifted) a second chance. This time I wasn't going to let anyone down, especially myself. I continued to work out hard right up until I had to leave to go to college. I knew where I'd gone wrong and I wasn't going to allow that to happen to me this time around. I knew not everyone got a second chance.

It was time for the football players to report to Alfred for conditioning practice and I got there about two weeks before actual school started. Unlike my first college experience, this time I showed up at school with a big black duffel bag, a suitcase, and one garbage bag of clothes. When I arrived, I met all my teammates and introduced myself, having a very similar experience to what I'd encountered at Dean. "Are you the same Leroy Collins who broke the New York state rushing record?" I was happy to hear I was known but it was a sad realization to understand that I'd almost lost it all.

We went out for our first practice and I started off slow as I was still unsure about my knee and the last thing I wanted to do was tear it again. I felt like I wasn't giving it my all in practice and I recognized my need to trust that I was okay. I knew I had to just get out there and play the game like I knew how to play it. I started to gradually challenge my knee by making sharp cuts and hitting top speed. I would do that constantly just to build the idea in my head that my knee was going to be okay and I could shake this mental block I had.

It was time for all the students to report to school for the start of the new year and things went much like I had remembered at Dean as students arrived with a car full of things; TVs, VCRs, video games, vacuums, microwaves, phones, answering machines—you name it, they had it. I was in the hallway doing pushups when I saw this pretty, older lady carrying things up the stairs so I stopped what I was doing and ran over to help. I helped her carry some of the things upstairs and noticed this girl with her who I assumed to be her daughter. She was the most beautiful girl I'd ever seen. It was obvious that they could use the help and I was anxious to help in whatever way I could. I held the door and helped carry heavy things up the stairs for them. I had to get to know this girl. She had the most beautiful, polite voice.

I introduced myself and even went so far as to ask her if she had a boyfriend. She told me she did but I didn't even care. From that point on I tried to ask her out to every school event just to be around her. I'd never felt like that before about anyone. Some time went by and I found myself wanting to hang out with her. I told her one night that I liked her. I just felt something was special about this girl unlike anyone I'd ever known. I invited her to football practice so I could impress her with some of my athletic skills but I never performed well when she came around. I think I was nervous because I never fumbled or dropped passes before. I only did those things when she came around. I felt like my hand was forced one day after a scrimmage. "I'm really a good football player, you know," I tried to emphasize in case she had any doubts. I found myself telling her all my records so she'd believe I was as good as I said I was, since she had yet to see it for herself. I think she believed me. Guys used to make fun of me because they knew I was trying to impress her and it seemed the more I tried, the more I messed up. But she hung around and got the chance to see me play for real. She would come out and hang with me and the guys and something about being around her just felt right.

o o o

I was feeling good about how things were going. I was playing football again and doing well, I'd found the girl of my dreams, and I was doing well academically. Then one day everything changed. I started to pick up some of the bad habits I thought I'd left behind at Dean. I thought I was strong enough to hang around people who smoked and could resist, but later one night I discovered I wasn't as strong as I thought I was. I ended up smoking with some friends, and looking back, it all happened so fast. It was like I forgot about what had happened to me back at Dean. It's crazy how life can change so fast through things that seem like such little decisions at the time. I was back hanging out and smoking weed with teammates. I started feeling awful again and needed a way out. I prayed and asked for help because I didn't want to go through this again and I didn't want to go through it alone. I knew I didn't want this for my life. I had a great opportunity in front of me and I didn't want to blow it.

God answered my prayers in the form of my girlfriend who loved me. She asked me if I would stop smoking weed, pointing out that I had too much to lose and it wasn't like me to smoke in the first place, she felt. She was right, and it felt good for someone to love me as much as she did and give me the encouragement I needed to stop smoking. I thanked God for her repeatedly because it was with her love and encouragement that I was able to stop smoking and find new faith and vision on my path to the NFL.

○ ○ ○

Suddenly it felt like the most amazing time of my life. I got to spend time with someone who made me feel like the most important person in the world, and I loved her dearly. I was doing well in school and I was dominating on the football field.

I was (and still am) so thankful I had a second chance to do the right thing and stay on my path.

One day as I looked at our football schedule I noticed we were slated to play Dean Junior College. I knew it was my fault that I was expelled from Dean my freshmen year, but there was something in me that wanted to show them I was ready to play and really show them what they'd lost. We were traveling to Dean to play them on their home turf and I knew it was going to feel weird and carry a lot of emotions. That place was where my life was turned upside down. In the long run it seemed that perhaps getting expelled was a blessing for me but I was still hurt that I'd been told to leave. If I stayed there no telling what would've happened to me. I'm grateful that I was removed from that situation. I wasn't hearing that small voice anymore but I truly believed God was guiding me somehow in getting me out of a bad situation.

When we arrived at Dean I saw a lot of the players from the previous year; my old teammates. Everybody welcomed me with open arms and we were exchanging jokes as I told them I was going to gain a thousand yards on them, and they told me they were going to break me and be sure I wouldn't clear so much as one hundred yards. We all laughed; it was all in good fun. I was happy to see some of my old teammates. I'd become good friends with some of them, especially my old roommate. We beat them that night and I had a great game. I rushed for over one hundred yards and scored three touchdowns. The final score was 45–25.

∘ ∘ ∘

I was having an amazing season averaging over one hundred yards and a couple of touchdowns a game. I started receiving letters of interest from D-1 colleges and that really boosted my confidence, making me work even harder in school and in football. I held Alfred's school record for rushing and since it was only their second season I didn't really have much of a challenge. Now that the season was over with I wanted to work out so I could come into the next season a bigger, faster, stronger running back. I started looking at colleges myself and the school I really wanted to talk with was Florida State. I sent them a letter of introduction with my stats and a video of my games, hoping it would get in the right hands. I'd lost the number I had for Coach Bowden so when I'd call the school I could never get him. I left him many messages. I was convinced that if he just watched my tape I thought they would consider me. While I waited I did my best to remain focused and I made sure I didn't fall back into any of my old habits. The school year was coming to an end and I was excited to have a break from school but not so happy about being away from my girlfriend. She had become my rock—her strength and love for me helped pull me through when I was weak. She was truly a godsend. We made plans to see each other as much as we could over the summer and I also made plans to train every day. I wanted to come back bigger and faster yet.

○ ○ ○

The summer went by fast and I took advantage of every day of it. I was ready to play some football. I'd gained a few pounds and I believed I was few steps faster. I couldn't wait for the chance to showcase my skills. We went in early for preseason training and the coaches noticed that I was coming in a little bigger. I started the season off good, picking back up from where I'd left off last year. The highlight of my second season would be when I got the chance to play against my younger brother, the same brother

I'd been in a car accident with. He went to Hudson Valley, a little community college not far from Hudson, and he had been a star linebacker in high school. Timing was such that we only played with each other for one season in high school, but now we would have the chance to play against each other in college.

My mother came to the game and she didn't know who to cheer for with me and my brother being on the field at the same time but for opposing teams. He was a starting linebacker and I was the starting running back. It was his job to stop me and it was my job to not let him stop me. So, my mother would be in the stands yelling at us to stop hitting each other. At one point I heard her tell my brother to get off me when he made a tackle and she told me not to run into my brother "like that." I assured her she had nothing to worry about. I was going to protect him, but I had to show him I was still the bigger brother.

It was fun playing against my younger brother. He was a great linebacker but I don't think he knew what he was up against when he stood on the other side of the ball from me. He claimed he was taking it easy on me, but we will never know. I was just wondering what was running through my mother's head as she watched her two boys playing against each other on the football field when less than fifteen years earlier she had been looking at us in the street, believing we were dead after we'd been run over by a truck. I wish I could've been in her mind that day just to see what she was thinking now. My mother is a very strong woman and she has always been my inspiration. My mother and girlfriend got along very well and that was important to me to have the two special women in my life get along so well and love each other.

o o o

This season was coming to an end and I now had letters flooding in from colleges all over the country. I felt so blessed to be in the position I was now in and I knew I owed my life to the Lord. My life had completely turned around and it seemed like everything was going right for me. I had enough credits to receive a scholarship, so now all I needed to do was choose a school. I went on a few college visits and the one I enjoyed the most was Syracuse University. They really wanted me but they wanted to change my position; I was a running back (and a pretty good one) and they wanted to recruit me to be a cornerback or safety. I didn't understand that until the recruiter explained it all to me. He said I had quick feet and I could easily switch to one of those positions. I didn't like the idea of switching my position when I knew I was so good at what I'd been doing all along. Syracuse was stacked at running back so they wanted my abilities to move quick and run fast. It wasn't a good sale for me. I didn't feel confident about Syracuse's plan so I declined their offer.

I decided to go with a different approach when choosing a school, where I was now checking to see how many running backs a school had before I chose it. I was contacted by Utah State college. They said they had watched my film, thought I was a very good running back, and they wanted to offer me a scholarship. I thought about it for a few days and I looked at their running back situation. This was a school that needed running backs! I accepted their offer and would now be set to play football for Utah State. I was waiting to receive the scholarship to sign but instead I received a phone call from the coaches. They called me to tell me that they were no longer coaching at Utah State, but now they were coaching at the University of Louisville. They also told me they wanted to fly me to Louisville for a visit. I was so happy

I couldn't even believe this was happening to me. I called my mother and told her the good news. She was so proud of me she started thanking Jesus for blessing me, rejoicing over the phone.

It was obvious that I'd have to fly to get to Louisville, and I'd never flown before. I was terrified of flying after watching all the airplane movies. As a kid, I swore that I'd never fly as an adult. "Coach," I said, "I've gotta admit I've never flown before. I'm not so sure I can do it."

"If you want to play in D-1 bad enough you'll find a way, son. You'd better get used to it because they fly to all their away games."

It was funny that I'd never thought about any of this until he brought it to my attention. I realized I had to find some courage and get on the plane, and I knew I'd have to do it alone. On the day I had to fly I woke up praying that everything would go right and the flight would arrive safely. I went to the store and I bought a trial-size bottle of NyQuil so I could sleep the entire way there—that was my plan anyway.

My girlfriend drove me to the Rochester airport and I drank my bottle of NyQuil hoping I didn't fall asleep before my flight boarded. It was my first time in an airport so my girlfriend had to help me check in and check my bags. As I walked to the waiting area I thought about how much I'd grown over the course of just a year and I knew I owed a lot of that to my girlfriend for the love she had shown me and the support that couldn't be ignored. My mother's relentless fight and faith was one of the reasons why I was in an airport waiting to go visit a D-1 school. She too had opened the door for me to have this opportunity. When others wanted me to follow the status quo, my mother refused for me to be anything other than great. She didn't want anyone else to determine our futures; she wanted us to determine the future for ourselves.

I was sitting there waiting for my flight and was starting to get drowsy when I heard them call my flight. My heart started racing as I walked toward my gate. I gave the attendant my ticket and headed toward the airplane. I started reciting 121 Psalms, finishing the prayer as soon as I made it to the plane. There in the door stood the pilot and flight attendants, the people who would hopefully deliver me to Louisville in one piece, I thought. They greeted me warmly and the pilot said, "Don't worry, you'll be okay," as if he could read my mind. It was weird that he felt the need to say that to me, but for some reason it actually did make me feel a little calmer.

I had a window seat so I closed the shade and waited for takeoff. The plane taxied to the runway and we sat there for a while. I'm not sure what the holdup was but we were there waiting and I fell asleep. When I woke up about an hour and a half later we were in the air. I panicked for a second before recalling what was going on and regaining my composure. There was an older lady sitting next to me who had fallen asleep with her head on my shoulder and I didn't want to wake her up so I just sat there while she slept. I could open the window without disturbing her so I focused on looking out and my eyes landed on the most beautiful thing I'd ever seen. We were above the clouds and I could see the sun far off in the distance among blue skies. The clouds looked like huge cotton mountains and the sky was like the ocean. It was so beautiful I forgot all about how scared I was of flying. The woman on my shoulder woke up and apologized. I told her it kept me calm so she shouldn't worry about it.

We reached Louisville and were going in for the landing. As we were descending I started seeing buildings and fields and highways rushing toward us and it felt amazing to see the land from this position where everything seemed so small. I thought I was doing fine until I heard a loud screeching noise and a big thud. I was shaken up and the lady next to me told me it was the wheel coming down for landing. I felt silly and a little embarrassed for reacting the way I did, but I explained it was my first time flying and this was like nothing I'd ever experienced before.

When I exited the plane there was a guy standing there holding a sign with my name on it and he wore a Louisville Cardinals jacket. I'm not going to lie—I felt like Michael Jordan when I saw that sign with my name on it. Someone was holding a sign just for me?! I identified myself and went with him as he took me to the Cardinals stadium. I met the coaches and they took me on various tours of the school. I got a chance to meet some of the players and I met the tallest human being I'd ever seen in my life. He was a lineman and I told him I was a running back and thinking about coming to Louisville. He laughed a little and said, "You better beef up."

I was 5 ft. 11 in., 170 pounds, and the Louisville roster was showing that their smallest running back was 5 ft. 7 in., and 190 pounds, with the biggest being 6 ft 2 in., and 240. I guess I had some work to do if I was planning on making my mark among these guys. I told the coaches I was very interested in attending Louisville and I gave them a verbal commitment.

As my visit was ending and the coaches told me I would be receiving a scholarship and it would be delivered to Alfred for me to sign and return. I could then make solid plans to report to spring camp in January of 1998. I went back to Alfred and tied up a couple of loose ends to prepare myself for graduation. I was onto another chapter in my life. It was hard to think that I wouldn't have my girlfriend with me in Louisville to share this experience, but we planned to see each other as often as we could.

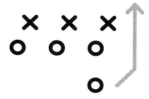

D-1 Scholarship

The day my scholarship letter came in I didn't waste a minute signing it. I was now officially a Louisville Cardinal.

I did it, I'm on my way to Louisville. That was my thought that day as I reminded myself about how I'd always been told you can do anything if you just believe—and believe is exactly what I'd done. I'd faced a few challenges and hit a few stumbling blocks along the way but I never gave up. I fell down a few times but I got back up because I believed. The old proverb says fall down seven times and get up eight—and that's exactly what I'd done once again in my life.

One of my old friends I was now leaving behind told me I could take my blinders off now because I'd made it. I had to explain to him that I wasn't done just yet. "This is a big step toward my dream," I said, "but I don't 'make it' until I've signed a contract with the NFL."

Picture day University of Louisville

1998

A week before I was set to leave my family had a small get-to-gether and shared some of our more meaningful moments of our lives thus far. I realized something that night as we were all gathered around the kitchen together—we didn't have much growing up. We were probably borderline poor (or poor) but my siblings and I never really knew it because we all had so much love for each other. Love really does overpower money and things any day, I realized.

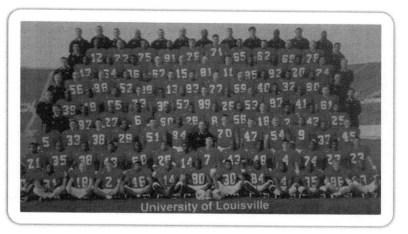

University of Louisville team pictures

1998

Winter break of 1998 was over and it was time for me to report to Louisville. My family hopped in the car and we all headed south. It was a long ride but I was thrilled to have everyone with me as I started this new chapter in my life and moved closer to my dream. When I made it to Louisville it was like the campus had turned into a ghost town. There was nobody there. The football team was the only group who had to report early to prepare for the spring season. I was nervous but I was really ready to get things started.

Once my parents and siblings left I attended a team meeting where the players and coaches all met. It was so exciting sitting in a room with a bunch of guys that I had probably watched on TV—and now I was going to have the opportunity to play on TV with them myself!

I felt pumped after the meeting and I went to get something to eat. I only had a few dollars and the cafeteria for the players wasn't set to open for a few more days. I called my mother and explained the situation. I didn't have any money and I was starving. She said she was going to send me some money but I knew it was going to take a few days and I literally didn't have anything. Not feeling as if I had much of a choice, the next day I went to the head coach and asked him if I could borrow a few dollars to buy some food with the sure intent of paying him back right away. "Of course—don't worry about it," he said. And he gave me twenty dollars. I went right to the store and bought not only some sandwich meat and bread but as many packs of Ramen noodles I could buy. While it wasn't exactly a glamorous start to my new life, at least I was here.

○ ○ ○

That next day we started early morning conditioning to prepare our bodies for spring ball. The morning workouts they called MAT drills were mandatory for all players. I had been conditioning all my life (pretty intensely) so I didn't think this would be much different from what I had been doing all along. Turns out I was wrong. It was one of the hardest things I'd ever been put through.

When I walked out onto the field for MAT drills I noticed there were five garbage cans set in various areas of the football field; one in each corner of the field and one right in the middle. There was also a lot of training equipment scattered all over the field and set up in various stations. The main instructions we got from Coach was for all of us to plan on working hard and above all else, don't throw up on his field (I now realized what the garbage cans had been set up for). "If you're going to be sick, you get yourself to a can and then jump right back in line and keep things moving," he said. Suddenly, I knew I wasn't in Kansas anymore. This was a whole new level of football.

We worked ourselves so hard that first day I didn't think I was even going to make it. I just hoped I had what it would take to be there. My resolve was strong and while I wasn't planning on quitting, I'll admit I was definitely close to passing out. I struggled through all the pain and the agony that first day and when I reflected on the day, I had to feel proud of the fact that I was still standing. But I knew I had to mentally prepare myself for the next two weeks if training was going to go on like this and I was still going to make it.

Believe it or not, it wasn't long before I started to enjoy the training. I was even looking forward to it because I felt myself getting stronger and faster. I looked at it this way: I had to work hard and enjoy the things that were going to get me to the place I wanted to be—whether that meant temporary pain or not—this was all going to get me where I wanted to ultimately be. I told myself I should never complain about any of that. I got my mind turned around to a positive place where I became somebody else in the weight room. I turned our team workout sessions into a fun, but still competitive, place to be. I loved sharing my energy with my teammates and positively affecting the team. I noticed that when I spoke loudly and offered extra encouragement my teammates seemed to gladly accept it and even joined in.

Our official practices and team meetings had begun a few weeks before the spring game and I was listed as the third-string running back. I was hoping that that would change over time once they all got a chance to see what I could do.

Practice wasn't going so well for me in the very beginning. We had a playbook that was like five hundred pages long and I found myself having trouble learning the plays fast enough to compete with the other running backs. I knew I had to study my playbook a little extra until I understood each play without hesitation. I just felt lost sometimes in practice and everything seemed to be moving so fast.

Then one day everything started to slow down. I remembered having this very same feeling when I was back in high school. I was still getting tossed around more than I was used to. Back in those days when I was running the ball in practice the coach used to yell at me and tell me to keep it up the middle and stop bouncing it outside. When I was in high school and junior college that had been my bread and butter. Coach was now telling me that I'd better learn to run up the middle if I was going to make it at this level. I tried to focus on that in practice but found myself still wanting to bounce it to the outside. I needed to work on that, but in general I felt good about where my level of fitness was going. I'd gone from weighing 170 to now weighing in at a solid 190 pounds of muscle within three months. I'd increased my size and my speed just in time for the spring game.

I had improved with my plays too, but I was still the third-string running back for now. I was hoping to impress the coaches in the spring game so I could move up on the depth chart. We broke our team up into two squads and I was the second-string running back for one of the teams. As I stood on the sideline and watched the other players I worked hard on envisioning what I was going to do when I get the chance to go in. The coach called me to go in and as I ran out on the field I started reciting the 121 Psalms to myself. The quarterback was telling us the play and I listened intently, ready to do my job. After we broke the huddle I finished my prayer. This would be a running play to me. As soon as I got the ball, a hole opened and I bounced it to the outside and picked up about twenty yards for my team. I was very happy about that, believing I'd done something special. When I got to the sideline the coach told me to stop bouncing it outside; the middle was there. "Stay up the middle!" he said. That was a blow to my ego. I'd had the longest run out of all the running backs, thought I'd done well, and I was getting yelled at for bouncing it outside. It was a little confusing as I wanted to know why the coach wasn't happy about the yards I'd just picked up. I was hoping to impress all the coaches in the spring game and already it seemed I'd just made things worse.

Later on, I talked to the coach to get his take on my performance of the spring game. He said I'd done well, but once again he reminded me that I needed to keep the ball up the middle. The linemen had the job to open holes for me and I had to start trusting my linemen and running the holes. I saw why he was upset—not because I was running outside it but because I wasn't letting the linemen do their jobs. I understand now and I planned to work on that and continue to focus on my playbook.

○ ○ ○

It was the end of the school year and we all went home for the summer but we had to return early for preseason practice. I only had two weeks at home until I had to return to Louisville for summer school and get ready for the season. I was coming into this season weighing two hundred pounds; I'd gained thirty pounds since starting at Louisville in January. I was also running faster than I ever had in my life. When we ran our forty times I clocked at a 4.27 unofficially, and 4.31 unofficially. I had the second fastest time on the team. I was beat out by a receiver who had the fastest start I'd ever seen in my life. I was just so anxious to see what I could do in a real Division 1 game. Our first game versus Kentucky was set to be about a week away and I found out that our game was going to be on TV. I called everybody who I had a phone number for to let them know we were going to be on TV and they needed to watch us play against the Kentucky Wildcats. I still was listed as the third-string but I was hoping I got some playing time.

Arriving the day before the game we all stayed at a hotel, having team meals and team meetings and walk-throughs. I felt like a superstar; getting royal treatment was something I wasn't used to. I honestly couldn't sleep the night before our first game. Just as with the spring game, I was hoping I could do something to impress the coaches enough that I could move up the depth chart.

Game day morning we had to meet in a conference room for breakfast and once we'd all fueled up on breakfast we had to go to our rooms to get all our gear and meet in yet another conference room for meetings and walk-throughs. Getting our strategy together and getting pumped up at our meeting, we all loaded onto the bus to head to the stadium. The ride there was nothing short of amazing. To say we were escorted by local law enforcement was an understatement—we had two officers in front of us and two officers behind us. I was sitting there in amazement gazing out the window with my Walkman on listening to Phil Collins's *In the Air of the Night*. The lyrics rang true for me: *I've been waiting for this moment for all my life*. And now it was here.

Coach helped us navigate our way through the stadium as this was our first game in this new venue. I was feeling psyched when we went to the locker room to get geared up and get our ankles taped so we could get out on the field to warm up. I eagerly put my football pants on and we anxiously went out on the field. It was a good crowd—maybe forty to fifty thousand people. We went through our warm-ups and walk-through before going back inside the locker room to get our full gear on. I got suited up and started to envision what I wanted to happen in the game—positive imagery had served me well in the past and I hoped this would be no different.

Coach gave a pregame speech and we headed to the field together as a team. As we made our way through the tunnel the roar of the crowd was overwhelming as we could hear people chanting our names before we even hit the field, "Cardinals! Cardinals!" Coming out of the tunnel my eyes lit up when I saw the stadium full of so many people. It was so overwhelming all I could do was just break down and cry. I was jogging into the stadium with tears in my eyes and I said, "Thank you, Jesus, I made it." I got to the center of the football field and took a moment to look around the stadium, realizing I needed a moment to take it all in to understand the multitude of people who had come to see us play. I felt this big surge of undeniable energy and just yelled out loud with joy.

We practiced a few plays and then we ran to the sideline for the National Anthem. While they started singing, I started saying my prayer, 121 Psalms, while walking to the sideline as it was almost game time. After the Anthem it was time to play and all I kept thinking about was how I was going to be on TV and every person in the world would get to see me. Me—Leroy Collins from Hudson, New York!

I was just so amazed about how excited the people in the stadium already seemed to be—the atmosphere was electric unlike anything I'd ever experienced. The closest I'd been to that much energy in any one place had been during my high school state championship when I'd played in the Syracuse Carrier Dome. All I could hope for now was the chance to play.

Kentucky jumped on us quick. They had a quarterback who was very good; one rumored to be a serious contender for the Heisman. I'd read up on this guy before the game and was excited to see him play. I didn't want him to beat us but I wanted to see what greatness looked like. I was always fascinated with greatness, always studying it. My coach in high school would always tell me, "If you want to be great, you've got to do what great people do." He also gave me wise words of advice on life in general: "Great people leave a blueprint; all I have to do is follow it and you yourself will be great one day." I really took those words to heart. Reading about greatness is one thing and having the opportunity to be in its presence and watching it unfold was incredible.

We won the toss of the coin and decided to receive the kick. We were on offense first. I was on the sideline just pacing back and forth. I really needed to get in the game to shake some of this nervousness off, I knew. I just wasn't used to standing on the sideline while the offense was out there playing. They stopped us on our drive. We kicked the ball to them and were able to stop them from scoring a touchdown on their first possession but they did get a field goal. With the score 3–0 we got the ball back, and then marched down the field to score our first touchdown. Now the score is 7–3 we are ahead. The new era of Louisville football is looking promising so far. Kentucky gets the ball back and started to look like they were creating a rhythm that was unstoppable. Kentucky marched down the field to get their first touchdown of the day. Kentucky took the lead with the score at 10–7. It was late in the first quarter and the coach called me over to let me know I was going in. I was really about to get in the game. As I was running to the huddle I really hoped my family was watching me on TV.

I stood in the huddle and focused on what the quarterback was calling. The quarterback called a run play to me. I started to freak out but wanted the ball. We break the huddle and headed to the line of scrimmage. The quarterback calls the cadence and hands the ball off to me on our 24-yard line. I was immediately met by tacklers and lost five yards on the play. It all happened so fast I wasn't even able to get my feet under me to make a move. Wow! The way they bounced on me I was not expecting. We went back to the huddle and my next play was a pass play that I had to block on. I really wanted to make up for that five yard loss. I walked to the huddle and started to envision what I wanted to happen if I got a chance to run again. I didn't get my chance on that possession because the drive ended in a punt to Kentucky. We stopped Kentucky on their next possession and they had to punt the ball to us. I went back on offense and was hoping the play was coming to me so I can make up for my negative run play. I got my wish; the ball was coming to me. Time to make this right. The quarterback got through his cadence and yelled "hut . . ." I ran and grabbed the ball I saw nothing but endzone. My eyes opened up so wide. The hole was so big you could have driven a truck through it. But only for a second. That big hole closed very fast but I was able to gain four yards which made me feel a little better than my previous carry. I was in on offense with a few pass plays in which I was blocking, But it was third down with six yards for a first down and they called a pass play to me. I wanted to get this first down so bad. The last thing I wanted to do was drop the first pass thrown to me under these circumstances. The quarterback hiked the ball, I ran my route, turned my head to look at the quarterback, and he threw me the ball. I reached out for the ball but started to turn up field looking for the first down before I had full possession of the ball. The ball bounced off my fingertips and hit the ground. I was devastated. This was not how I envisioned it. We had to punt the ball off once again. This really hurt me. The team and coaches were counting on me and I let them down.

I was simultaneously angry and embarrassed. I couldn't believe how quickly things changed and that I dropped a pass at a critical time on national TV. I honestly didn't think the coach was going to let me back in. I was already third-string, I wasn't getting much playing time as it was, and now I'd dropped a pass on a third down. I didn't think I had a chance and I was ready to throw in the towel. I was not used to gaining only three or four yards at a time. I was thinking to myself: *Are these guys really that good or was my whole career average?* I was shocked at how good they contained me and only allowed me to gain a few yards at a time. We ended up losing that game 68–34. The KU quarterback had thrown for 498 yards and 7 touchdowns—and he'd only played three quarters.

Our Louisville team lost nine games in a row the previous season with a record of 1–10. Then we started this season off with a 68–34 loss? Such a defeat didn't give our fans much faith in the new coaching staff or new signees like me. I was hoping I could do something to turn things around, and instead of delivering on that, I'd dropped passes and lost yards. I thought they'd never trust me with the ball again. I was so angry and disappointed in myself when I walked back into that locker room. I seriously considered the fact that it could be my very *last* time in any locker room because I was going to quit.

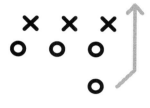

Things Are about to Change

I went to my apartment that night and thought about what I was going to do, and if I quit, where I was going to go. Ironically, just at the time I needed it most, I got a phone call from my mother. "I saw my baby on TV!" she said excitedly. "But from what I could see them show on the jumbo screen, it looked like you were throwing a fit . . . What was all that fuss about?"

I explained what had happened and told her that I might be leaving Louisville. I didn't think I was cut out for this.

"Now come on, Leroy. You know you're no quitter. How could you forget all you've been through just to get there? You've worked so hard in every possible way; you can't be serious."

"No, Mom, really. I think I'm serious. I feel like I screwed up when it really mattered. I'll never make it off third-string playing like I did today, that's for sure."

"Well you know what you have to do . . . You just have to work harder if you want things to change. You have a dream,

Leroy, and dreams don't come easy. You know you need to dig deep and besides that, don't ever let them see you hurt like you did today on that big jumbo screen—you're so much better than that!"

Mom's words sparked something in me that night. I gave myself a long hard look in the mirror and told myself I was going to work harder than everybody else and I was going to accomplish great things. End of story.

In thinking back over my mistakes that day I realized the reason I bounced my runs to the outside was because I was afraid of getting hurt. I'd spent my whole life hearing people tell me I shouldn't do this, or shouldn't do that, because I'd get hurt. I didn't know any of that had ever affected me but it was clear it had. This technique I'd developed to protect myself while moving the ball may have worked in high school and in junior college because I was so much faster than everybody else, but I couldn't do it at this level. I would need to change my style, and even more than that, I'd have to learn not to be afraid anymore.

I decided to revise my running style to be more aggressive—fearless even. I knew I had to make an impression so I went to practice with an attitude. I told myself I was going to run every play 100 percent without hesitation. I wasn't going to try to hurt my teammates but I had to break a fear that I'd been holding onto for a long time—I'd just never realized it. Entering into this new territory, I was nervous because I was now intentionally going to bang heads and no one knew it but me. There wasn't anyone who knew I was feeling this way but I knew they were all going to see a drastic difference in Leroy Collins's style once practice started.

I was doing warm-ups and stretches and the only thing that was running through my head before practice that day was "Go 100 percent." When we ran sprints, I ran them as fast as I could, holding nothing back. When it was time for hitting drills, I said, "Okay, here we go . . . Let's see what you got." We did a running back/linebacker drill where the running back chooses a hole and tries to get around or through two linebackers. When it was my turn to go I already knew that I wasn't going to make a move. I was going to run full speed into them and try to run through them. The quarterback gave me the ball and I ran as fast as I could into our linebackers. They hit me so hard I thought I'd separated my shoulder but I didn't go down right away. I tried to get away until I was brought down, thinking that was the first time in my career that I had planned on running into a would-be tackler. Now I knew I could do it, and I'd need to do it again. I got back in line when the two best linebackers on the team were up next. I was at the end of the line but intentionally cut to the front so I could go against the two of them. They welcomed the challenge, having no idea that I wasn't interested in making a move and trying to get away from them. All I cared about was overcoming this fear that had been instilled in me when I was a little boy. The quarterback handed me the ball and I chose a hole, running at them as fast as I could before I hit the first linebacker. He bounced off me and went down, and the second linebacker hit me but I kept my legs churning and was able to pick up a few more yards before he brought me down. The other running back and linebackers were getting hyped up and cheering.

Something happened that day. I started changing the coaches' minds about me; I could see it. When we lined up to have an inner-squad scrimmage I noticed the coach was giving me more carries and paying me a little more attention. I ran like this for the rest of the week and couldn't wait to get a chance to run this same way in the game, hopeful that it would make a big difference for me.

Turned out we'd be having to travel next to Utah to play against the Utes, and I wasn't happy about that because I still wasn't confident about flying. Just as before, I made sure I got myself a little bottle of NyQuil to take before the flight. The bus drove us right up onto the runway that day so we could board the plane. I drank my bottle of syrup before I got on the plane so I could sleep once we took off. I walked to my seat, sat down, and started saying my prayers. The plane wasn't wasting any time getting in the air and it was very loud so I didn't get a chance to fall asleep right away. During our entire takeoff I didn't stop praying until the pilot said we were safe to remove our seatbelts. I will say this—it was definitely better to fly with teammates than alone. I felt a lot calmer during this flight than the one I'd taken to Louisville for my visit. I fell asleep shortly after takeoff but only slept a half hour because my teammates were loud. I listened to my Phil Collins song maybe ten times after we woke up to not only get me pumped up, but also to block out some of the noise.

When we got into Utah the plane had to make a turn and in the middle of the plane turning around it sounded like the engine shut down and we were just gliding for a second until it started back up. Most of us who noticed freaked out—and I was one of them. We landed safely in Utah and I said a "thank you, Jesus" prayer and exited the plane.

This was my first time being anywhere on the west coast. It was at times like this that I still found myself awed by the opportunity to see so many other parts of the country just to play football—states that I would've never had the chance to see if it wasn't for football. I felt so blessed to be given this opportunity and I was grateful to my mother for talking me out of quitting. She was right; I'm not a quitter, I'm a fighter.

o o o

On game day I was so ready to prove myself to the coaches and to remind myself of what I was really made of. I wasn't the starter but I'd been told by the coaches that I was going to get some playing time, so I should be ready. I ran through my pregame routine like I'd always done before games, ever since high school. I whispered my 121 Psalms to myself and thanked God for this opportunity.

Utah got a quick start on us that day, scoring two touchdowns in the first two minutes of the game. The score was already 14–0 and we hadn't even had the chance to drive the ball yet. When we finally did get the ball, we scored quickly as well. I was sitting on the sideline just waiting for my chance to get in. I had a plan to block and run harder than I ever had, and when I got in the game I stuck to my plan. I ran hard with no hesitation and everybody that attempted to tackle me felt my determination. I could sense the coaches starting to feel more confident in my abilities and the skills I'd been working on. They called a run play for me on a third down. I was shocked when they called on me to get the first down. I was honored and I wasn't about to let them down. The quarterback handed me the ball and I hit one guy, shaking him off before I hit another guy, did a spin move to get away from another defender, and ran through two more players for the first down. I was tackled at the first down mark and when I stood up I felt a surge of power shoot through my body. I felt totally in control and all I wanted to do was run the ball again. I got a few more carries that game and I ran with authority. Despite my efforts, and what I felt was a good personal performance, we lost that game 28–14, but not because they were a better team. They just got a quick jump on us and we ran out of time before we were able to come back.

That loss was our team's tenth in a row and it wasn't looking good for us as a whole, but the coaches were really impressed with my performance. The running back coach even came to me and congratulated me on my hard work. "That was some good running out there," he said. "You really stepped it up." I didn't know what was to come from his comment but I was hoping it was an indication that they'd start to give me a bigger role in subsequent games. Later that week in practice my wish came true. The coach approached me and said they were going to make me the starter for that week's game. I looked the coach in the eyes and thanked him, assuring him I wouldn't let him down. I walked away, dropped down to my knees, and started crying and thanking God for this opportunity. This was what I'd been working so hard to hear. I knew it was coming; I just didn't know when. I saw my opportunity playing out . . . I saw myself as the starter, and I saw myself leading this team as I knew only I could do. The coaches were now giving me the keys and I had to do something with them.

o o o

Now that I was named the starter I was playing a bigger role in our wins or losses. I wanted to do more for the guys then just help by running the football. I wanted to inspire my teammates and mentally stimulate them. I wanted to help them all see that while we may have been 0–2, we were warriors, and if we linked together we could dominate any battle. Formulating a plan to motivate my teammates, I went to the hardware store and bought some chain links for all the players and asked them to lace the links through their shoestrings. I also wrote a coinciding poem for the team in which I was also talking to myself. I called the poem "I Challenge You." The poem was telling us that we should come together as a team and play with courage in order to finish the game strong. It read as follows:

I challenge you to play sixty minutes of football until the last whistle is blown,

I challenge you to come on the field with courage and leave the courage at home.

I challenge you to play for your team, and for no one else

I challenge you

Now challenge yourself

The poem really moved us all. My teammates all thanked me for putting it together and for spurring us all on. Everyone now felt ready to play.

We had to travel to Illinois to play the Illinois Fighting Illini next. I'd watched a lot of film on these guys with hopes of having a great game. I'd heard about a linebacker they had who was one of the best in the country and I scouted him to memorize his weaknesses and to study his strengths. On game day I sat in the locker room with my eyes closed and focused on what I wanted to do in the game. I said my prayers and walked on the field with courage and confidence. It took me the first couple plays of the game to get my footing but I was running hard and it seemed like no matter what hole I ran to, there was someone there waiting for me. I would pick up a yard or two but I wasn't performing at the level I was hoping. Still, I never slowed down. I kept looking over my shoulder thinking the coaches were going to pull me out because I wasn't producing much in the way of yardage. It was third and six and the quarterback called a swing pass to me. I ran out to receive the pass but a linebacker jumped at the ball and tipped it. The ball was just floating in midair with other Illinois players around it. I stopped and ran back toward the ball to snatch it out of the air, cutting through two guys and running for a first down. I looked over to our bench and I saw my coaches all cheering and clapping, yelling, "Way to go!" I felt good about that and didn't feel the need to look over my shoulder so much so I was producing more yards. I think that was the spark that we all needed that day. We drove the ball down the field and I ran it down to the one-yard line. I was hoping I'd scored but they stopped me before I could get in. On my way back to the huddle I told myself that if they called my number again I was going to score. The quarterback called a run play for me and the lineman told me to follow him—he would get me in. They snapped the ball and I got it and dove in for my first D-1 touchdown. I was so happy I ran off to the sideline where all the guys were giving me high-fives and hugs. Everyone was so happy for not only the team, but also for me personally as well. I got down and thanked Jesus, just as I'd always done. We ended the game strong and won 35–9. I ended the game with 159 yards and 3 touchdowns. I had a 48-yard touchdown that I broke right up the middle and high-stepped into the end zone. I also had a 52-yard touchdown that was a little tougher where I'd had to break a few tackles before I broke to the outside and dragged a guy into the end zone with me. The guys and coaches were so happy that we'd finally broken our 10-game losing streak.

That win gave us so much confidence that we went on to win a few more games right in a row. We played Boston College and we beat them 52–28. I had another impressive game—I'd scored two touchdowns and run for over one hundred yards. We continued to be victorious, taking on the Cincinnati Bearcats and defeating them 62–19. We really found some momentum and we were on a three-game winning streak, now scoring at will.

We were really feeling good when we had to travel to Southern Mississippi to play the Number One defense in the country. I was ready for the challenge. I wanted to test my skills against the best and this was my chance. When the game started, Mississippi jumped on us early. Twelve minutes into the game they had us at 21–0; we were just unable to move the ball. They called a running play to me and I got the ball thanks to my linemen who opened up a hole big enough to fit a truck through. I took off down the field for about thirty yards. I had one guy to beat and I went to stiff arm him but he slapped my hand down and tackled me out of bounds. I was so angry—my team really needed this in order to get back in the game. I eventually ended up scoring but we lost this game 56–21. It was a familiar story; much like what we'd encountered back in Utah. We had allowed them to get ahead by too much too early and we'd run out of time when we were trying to come back.

That was a tough loss but we didn't waste time dwelling on it for long because we were going to play the team with the best record in our conference, traveling to New Orleans to play the Tulane Green Wave. They had an undefeated record and were ranked twenty-fourth in the nation. Despite our 3–3 record, if we beat them we had a chance at being top in our conference. We were still sour from the loss to S. Mississippi so we were ready to play our hearts out and gain this victory. As it turned out it was a pretty close game the whole way; we were evenly matched teams. Our quarterback was connecting on almost every pass and I was having a decent day running the ball.

Early in the fourth quarter we were down 28–19. We had an amazing drive. We drove the ball down to the fourteen-yard line. They gave me the ball a few times in hopes of getting a first down. I was stopped from getting a first down on my attempts. It was fourth down with one yard to go. The coach trusted in me to get the first down so he called yet another play to me. I didn't want to let him down, especially after he saw I was stopped on the two previous plays, but he called my number again. We broke the huddle and the quarterback called the cadence. He handed me the ball, I immediately went airborne. As I got the highest point of my jump I clearly crossed the first down mark but on my way down a player from the opposite team put his helmet right on the ball and popped it out. The ball went so high in the air I was able to turn and watch it come down as players piled on top of me preventing me from getting the ball back. I was so devastated that I lost the ball after the hard work the team put in to get down there. I was also hurt that I let the coaches down after they trusted in me.

I walked to the sideline and the closer I got I could hear the coaches yelling, "Come on Leroy! Are you kidding me? Hold on to the ball." One of my teammates came up to me and patted me on the chest and said, "Pick your head up, we need you. We're still in the game, let's just get it back." I said, okay, but I really wasn't sure if the coaches would even let me back in the game. Tulane Green Wave took a lot of time off the clock, but we were able to stop them from scoring. We got the ball back with the score still 28–19, so we did have a chance. I went back out with the offense and I wanted to make up for the fumble. I wanted to put us in the lead. We ran a few plays and gained a few yards. Then the coach called a play to me. The quarterback got to hand me the ball and as I was receiving it from the quarterback, a player for the opposite team squirted through and knocked the ball out of my hand. The ball rolled and luckily one of our players recovered the fumble. All I could say to myself was not again, not again. This was not my day. The coach called me to the sideline and told me to take a seat. I was very upset, but I understood. Even though I'd never gotten taken out of a game because lack of performance, I had this one coming to me with the conference championship on the line. After my fumble and recovery the offense finished that drive with a field goal which made the score 28–22. We kicked the ball off to the Green Wave. We stopped them. I was cheering louder than I ever cheered before in my life.

We got the ball back and had a chance to go down the field and take the lead. The quarterback was on point with every pass and the receivers were catching some amazing passes. We got the ball inside the five-yard line with seconds left on the clock and we fell short on two incomplete passes. The time expired and we were handed another defeat.

On the way home, I must have gone over that play a hundred times. What could I have done differently to protect the ball a little more? I was beating myself up about it because we would've had a better chance at winning if I'd gotten that first down and not fumbled. In the game of football anything could've happened, there's no telling. I was upset for a long time and I had to snap myself out of it because I still had another half of the season to go. I couldn't go back and change something that had already happened so I had to learn from it and move on.

When we played Memphis, I knew we needed a win bad. Not just because we were on a two-game losing streak, but because we were playing at home and we couldn't afford another loss. We played our hearts out and it was a tough game but we won 35–32. I loved playing in front of the home crowd. They gave us a lot of love and support and were with us whether we won or lost.

o o o

One morning I woke up and there was a picture of me on the front page of *USA Today*. Wow, I thought. They were talking about my truck accident and my accomplishments now at Louisville. It was such an unexpected shock because I'd never been interviewed by anyone at that paper. A couple of days after the article came out one of my teammates said he had a friend who was an agent and wanted to talk to me. I wasn't sure what were the rules around that were this early in the season but I agreed to see him and told my teammate to set the meeting up.

A few days later my friend and I met the agent for dinner. He went right into his pitch, telling me how good he thought I was and making it clear that he wanted to represent me if I decided to come out that year. Prior to this very meeting, that thought hadn't even crossed my mind. For now, my mind had been set on becoming the best running back college football had ever seen. I planned on finishing the season and starting my workout program early so I could have a run at the Heisman Trophy. He told me he thought I would easily be one of the top running backs in the draft if I decided to come out that year. I was speechless.

My name and the NFL draft were in the same sentence.

o o o

I was thinking long and hard about going into the draft. I asked some trusted family members for advice. I was just so confused and afraid of making the wrong decision on my own. I really wanted to come back to school and set all kinds of records and make it to another championship, but I also wanted to take care of my mother for all the love and support she'd given me unconditionally for all those years. She sacrificed a lot in her life to make sure all of her kids were taken care of. I never would have even had a chance to play college football if it wasn't for her fighting for me every chance she had, even in times when she didn't full-heartedly agree with my wishes. She never stopped believing in me and I was looking forward to the day that I could give something back to her.

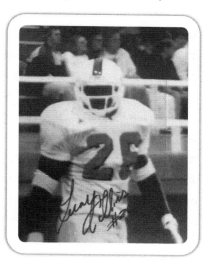

Louisville

1998

After much thought I told the agent I wasn't sure if I wanted to leave just yet. He encouraged me to think about it, and when

I was ready he wanted to represent me. I told him okay, but the truth was, I couldn't get it out of my head! This was my absolute dream—the very goal I'd set as a determined little kid, and it was standing right there in front of me when most people said it would be impossible.

I had more games to play so I had to get this notion out of my head for now. We went on to win the next three games against Western Kentucky, East Carolina, and Army. In the match-up against Western Kentucky I broke a school record with five touchdowns, and then I broke the one-thousand-yard mark against East Carolina. I was really proud of my guys. We managed to bounce back from a two-game losing streak to go on a three-game victory run only to lose two more and win four straight. We ended the season 7–4 and earned a bowl game, a very exciting accomplishment for the coaches and players. Back at the beginning of that season there was no way we had ever looked like we had a shot at a bowl game, but we beat the odds and turned things around, surprising even ourselves.

o o o

The bowl game was a few weeks away so I had time to train as well as time to think. I still just didn't know what do. I'd read stories about guys coming out as juniors and getting drafted high, and I'd also read stories about guys declaring for the draft as juniors and not getting drafted. Then to confuse matters even further, there were times where guys chose to not leave as a junior when they were a guaranteed top draft pick. It seemed those guys stayed for their senior seasons and then many had something happen, like a tear or break, and they were deemed never able to play again. There really were a lot of factors to consider and a lot of different scenarios to run through before I could make a solid decision.

I believed I was good enough to play in the NFL. I just wanted to be sure the timing was right and this was the smart decision for me to make. I asked my mother's opinion on me possibly going into the NFL and she made her position clear—she wanted me to graduate first. I reminded her that I had enough credits to graduate at the end of the year. Knowing her expectations of me would be met, she told me to do what I thought was right, and she suggested I seek advice from someone else since she didn't feel she was the right one to ask. (At least she was honest!)

As we prepared to travel to our bowl game the decision to declare myself up for the draft was heavy on my heart. I gave it up to God and asked Him to guide me and help me do the right thing. I knew I wanted to perform well in the bowl game so I had to clear my head and focus. This game was going to be nationally televised so I wanted to make sure I did everything right, knowing what was now at stake.

Before the game I sat quietly and visualized the game and how I wanted it to play out. I saw myself making good blocks, catching the ball, and running the ball with authority. At the start of the game I was confident we would win. I just had a feeling that it was going to be a good day.

Things didn't turn out quite the way I thought they would. I thought we would walk away with the victory but instead we lost that game like all of our losses during regular season. Once again, we ran out of time before we got a chance to come back. We had allowed the other team to get too far ahead too early.

We played well and I had an amazing game and had performed well. I just wish we'd had a victory attached to my stats. I rushed for over one hundred yards and scored three touchdowns and two-point conversions. I was so frustrated by the loss that I didn't even want to think about the NFL; or so I thought until I was approached on the field by a reporter asking me questions right after the game. After a few questions about the game itself he said, "What do you think, Leroy? Are you coming back next year?"

I was shocked by his line of questioning and I wondered what he knew. "I don't know," I said.

"Does that mean there's a chance you'll enter the draft?"

I must have looked like a deer in the headlights when I said, "Maybe."

It felt strange for a reporter to ask me that question. On my way to the bus I was shaking hands with all the people lined up waiting to tell us "good job," "heck of a season," and "better luck next year." Then, like something out of a movie, the agent that I'd been talking to earlier in the month handed me an envelope. I took the envelope and he disappeared into the crowd indicating he'd talk to me later. (Again, like something from a movie, right?) I got on the bus and when I opened the envelope it was full of a stack of one-hundred-dollar bills. I went to my teammate (the friend who had introduced us) and told him.

"He gave you the money because he wants to represent you if you decide to enter the draft," he said.

"Oh," I said, still staring at all this money that had been personally handed to me just moments before.

o o o

The next day there was a write-up in the paper that said, "Collins is entering the draft." How could this be? I knew I hadn't declared it. I wasn't even 100 percent sure yet if I was going to enter. But there it was in black and white, and it caused people to talk and wonder. As I read on I noticed my head coach's comment in the article. He was quoted in bold print, "Let him leave . . . Where does he think he's going?" I was so disappointed and angry with him. I couldn't believe he would say something like that after all the dedication and work I'd put in. He said those things to embarrass me (it worked) and to make me look worthless and dispensable. Seeing this brought back the same feelings I was having growing up as I tried to prove people wrong. When my coach said those things, it wasn't like he said it to me. He put me down to the whole community of Louisville. He had a bigger voice than my guidance counselor back in high school and a few different people I'd grown up with in my neighborhood. He had the country's ear, so after I read his comment I dug my heels in and declared myself for the draft. I felt like he'd slapped me in the face and I wasn't going to just roll over.

Of course, the only real reason I entertained the idea to enter the draft had been for my mother. She'd sacrificed her career and goals to take care of me for all those years. I went home for winter break still not sure if I had made the right decision because I'd really enjoyed my year at Louisville. But I had the opportunity in front of me and I told myself I might as well take it.

o o o

I was sitting at home one day and I received a call from my head coach. He told me to withdraw my name from the draft. I told him I wanted to go, and he said good luck and abruptly hung the phone up. His attitude only sparked me to start training harder to get prepared for the combine and the college pro day. "My agent" showed me different magazines and articles where NFL scouts had been saying good things about me and talking me up. I officially signed with agent D because I felt comfortable with him and my teammate knew him. I knew the combine was coming up soon and I was wondering when I was going to hear more about it. He told me the coach would have to request me because I was a junior and Coach J wouldn't request me. I didn't know I had to get requested to go because I had impressive running back numbers and I'd broken records on top of that. Since I wasn't requested by Coach J, I wasn't going to the combine.

I didn't know what I was going to do. My agent said he couldn't do anything about it because the coach had to request you and he wasn't answering any of his calls. My agent then told me we'd just have to wait for the college pro day. "There will be just as many teams at the college pro day as there were at the combine," he assured me. I felt a little better until pro day actually came around and the coach wouldn't let me attend that either. Now it came to me that he had it out for me and was really trying to prevent me from getting drafted. As far as I was concerned, he was trying to stop me from helping my mother, the woman who had put everything down to sit next to me night after night after night when I was in a coma. This man was trying to step between me and my dream to play in the NFL—the dream I'd had as a child when I wasn't able to walk.

"Does this seem fair?" I asked my agent one day. "Does it seem right to you that he can prevent me from working out in front of the NFL teams?"

"I hear what you're saying," he said. "Honestly, I've never seen anything like it before. I'll look into it."

My chances to be seen by the NFL were looking slim. The combine was over and the college pro day was gone, so what did

I have now? My agent contacted some teams that came to pro day just to see me, and they scheduled a private workout with me. My agent called and asked if I could train at the school, and they agreed. So, I drove to Louisville from Fredericksburg, Virginia, with my agent for a private workout for NFL teams.

I got to Louisville around 11:30 p.m. and my workout was scheduled for 10:00 a.m. the next morning. I tried to go to sleep fast so I could get some good sleep before the workout. That ended up not working out as I was up all night thinking about how my coaches were trying to sabotage my chance to play in the NFL. I couldn't believe this was happening to me.

I got a few hours of sleep, got up, ate some breakfast, and headed to the stadium. When I got there, I thought they were going to allow me to run for the NFL teams in the new training facility where they'd had the pro day. But instead they had me work out on the old rug turf outside in the foggy, damp weather. I felt so disrespected; things had changed for me in Louisville to the point where the coaches treated me like I was nothing. I was no better to them than trash. I was boiling on the inside but I tried not to show it because I had to perform in front of NFL teams for the first time.

I didn't run a good 40 that day but I did well on the drills. I ran my heart out, giving it everything I had overall. I thought I'd had an average workout; one that probably wasn't enough to impress the NFL scouts—I needed a do-over. I wasn't very happy about the environment and the treatment. I tried to reach out to some of the coaches but they all were unavailable so I just headed back home and told my agent I needed another workout with some other teams. The draft was coming up soon and I hadn't gotten the chance to perform well in front of the scouts.

I kept in contact with some of the players in Louisville and I told them what Coach J was doing to me. He was making it very hard for me to get looked at. My teammates told me he was making an example out of me. They also told me this wasn't his first time doing this to a player either. I started to panic—the draft was right around the corner. I asked my agent if he could contact other schools to see if I could work out in their facilities, and he contacted a school in Fredericksburg, Virginia, named Mary Washington. They were delighted to have me come work out at their school. Mary Washington didn't have a football team; it seemed they had every other sport, most notably, soccer. It was exciting news for them to have a potential NFL player work out at their school.

I had a few scouts come out to see me and I believed I'd performed better at this workout then I had at the one in Louisville. I ran a better 40 time now at 4.40. It still wasn't my best but it was impressive, nonetheless. The Miami Dolphins were one of the teams I worked out for. They were really impressed with my workout and with my season. The Dolphins' coach wanted to meet me in person, so the Dolphins flew me to Miami to see the facility and meet all of the coaches. I was just so amazed. I was thanking God the whole time despite what my college coaches were doing to me or saying about me. I was in the presence of a team that wanted to draft me.

When I got to the Dolphins facility I went to meet Coach JJ. We sat down and watched a few of my runs from previous seasons. Coach JJ was complimenting me on every run we watched. I was so excited. Then he said the words I was waiting to hear.

"We're looking to draft you on the Saturday draft—a week from now." I was so excited and ready to put all the frustration of this draft and working out for teams behind me. The draft was only a couple of days away. I was just so excited when I envisioned myself taking care of my mother. I was more excited that I might now be able to do for her now as she'd done for me for so long.

I was going to the NFL.

o o o

On draft day I woke up very nervous and excited. The suspense kept my stomach in knots all day. I had a few family members who came to my mother's house to support and share this excitement with me. First round of the draft started and I didn't know what to do with myself. Miami had a first-round pick that I thought for sure was going to be me. Miami traded up their first round so they only had the second round to the seventh round. I watched the entire first round on pins and needles. I compared myself to some of the guys who were drafted in the first round. I was on their level and in most cases above it. But yet I didn't get drafted in the first round. I knew I was a first-round player and I knew I should've been picked up in the first round but it was over. The only thing that was in my head was Coach J from Louisville was throwing my name in the dirt making me look bad. I had to calm myself down and just believe that Miami was going to draft me in the second round. Miami haven't had a draft pick yet because they gave up their first round. Second round came around and I could only watch it for a few minutes. Miami had two second-round picks they had on the eighth pick in the second round and they had the thirteenth pick in the second round.

When the second round started I couldn't watch. I had to leave the house so I went for a long walk and prayed. I got back to the house maybe a half hour later and I anticipated walking in to hear I'd been signed by the Miami Dolphins. But as I walked in the house and Miami was making their first pick, they chose a running back, and it wasn't me. I just kept the faith and hoped that pick number thirteen was going to be me. I stayed in the house and watched it this time. Miami's thirteenth pick came up and they picked another running back, and it wasn't me. This was getting old and I was just plain confused now. Miami had just picked two running backs so I didn't believe they were going to pick a third. Why would they?

I went into the bedroom and cried, asking God to just do His will; if it was meant for me, let it be so. If it's not meant to be, I'll follow you. The draft ended and my name hadn't been announced.

I was sad but not broken. I believe God was there to relieve me from this shock.

I talked to my agent and asked him what had happened. He told me not going to combine and pro day had really hurt my chance since teams base everything off the combine. Regardless of your season, if you have a good combine it will help your chances of getting drafted.

When the draft was over I started receiving phone calls from almost every team in the NFL. They wanted to sign me to a free agent contract. I chose to go to the Washington Redskins because it was within driving distance to my mother. I was grateful that in the end I'd have a chance to prove myself despite everything that had happened.

I'd had this vision as a little boy to go to the NFL, and I did it. I signed a contract and was now on an NFL team.

Let's see what's next . . .

One of my touchdowns in the carrier dome
during the state championship game

1994

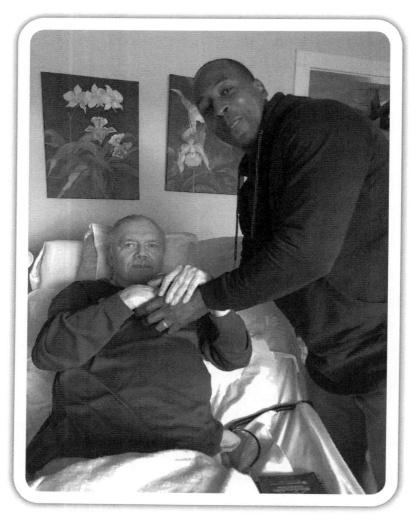

My visit with officer Larry Walker

2019

The Collins Family

2009

In life you are going to face many challenges.
Challenges that are going to make you want to give up.
Challenges that are going to make you even question your existence.
We must remember challenges are supposed to
make us stronger, make us wiser.

About the Author

Leroy grew up in Hudson, New York, the second of eight children. While in high school, he was the New York State rushing leader and broke the Section 2 rushing record in 1994. Collins went on to play football at Alfred State College and the University of Louisville. Following his NFL career with the Washington Redskins and Jacksonville Jaguars, he moved to Fulton, New York with his wife Kristen and three sons. Currently, he is a personal trainer, sports consultant, motivational speaker, Pop Warner Football coach, and community organizer. In addition, he is an active member of his church, where his faith has fostered his desire to give back to his communities. Leroy enjoys supporting others reach their potential and building relationships to build a stronger community as a team. In his free time he likes to spend time with his family coaching and supporting his sons in their own athletic endeavors. Leroy plans to continue writing his story to share with others in hopes of inspiring them to have the audacity to dream big.

Made in the USA
Middletown, DE
04 April 2022

63566959R00125